ROWING AND SCULLING

SKILLS

TRAINING

TECHNIQUES

Rosie Mayglothling

with Tristan Mayglothling

THE CROWOOD PRESS

First published in 2015 by
The Crowood Press Ltd
Ramsbury, Marlborough
Wiltshire SN8 2HR

www.crowood.com

© The Crowood Press 2015

Text illustrations and photographs © The Crowood Press

British Library Cataloguing-in-Publication Data
A catalogue record for this book is available from the British Library.

ISBN 978 1 84797 746 5

Acknowledgements
We would like to thank Rebecca Caroe at Row Perfect for supplying the ergometer sequence of rowing; Miriam Taylor, Katie James, Mark Hunter, Helen Glover and Heather Stanning who all helped with and appear in the action sequences; Phil Harfield, Mark Homer and Craig Williams for keeping us on track with the science and letting us ask them lots of questions; Pangbourne College for hosting some of the photo shoots and for their rowers who helped with the capsize drill; and thanks to Andy Smith, Patrick White and Eileen Langsley who supplied some of the photos. Finally a big thank you to Don Somner who supplied most of the photos and was very patient to ensure they were right for the book.

Tristan Mayglothling also played an enormous part in compiling this book. Tristan played as many sports as possible in his teens and finally came into rowing at the age of fifteen. He raced twice at Henley and represented England in the Home Countries event in Cork in 2003. After leaving school, he completed a BTec in sports studies, combining this with coaching rowing at a local school. He was appointed as the Chief Coach for juniors at Star Club and has coached at University and school level. He is once again combining his coaching at Cheltenham College with studying for a degree in sports coaching at the University of Gloucestershire.

Photographs by Don Somner

Typeset by Jean Cussons Typesetting, Diss, Norfolk
Printed and bound in Singapore by Craft Print International

CONTENTS

PART I

AN INTRODUCTION TO ROWING

Chris Martin and Mick Dawson complete their Pacific crossing under the Golden Gate Bridge in 2010.

required to accompany such a boat in the English Channel. Timed descents of the Thames and other short sea crossings, or combinations such as the London–Paris race, are becoming increasingly popular, with records being established and broken all the time. More important for most, however, is the satisfaction of completing a challenge beyond our previous experience.

Naval Boats, Sea Scouts, Sea Cadets and Sea Rangers

The Navy has traditionally relied on pulling boats to move men and goods to and from their ships, as did the merchant fleets that were trading to and from the UK. These boats are still used by the Navy, and also by allied groups such as the Sea Cadets, Sea Scouts and Sea Rangers. There are annual water festivals where the boats are raced, in addition to their use on a regular basis to develop teamwork and watermanship.

Surfboats

Originally hailing from Australia, surfboats can now be found around the south west coast of England. This exciting and fast growing sport has a European and International Association, with test matches held in different parts of the world. The surfboat specifications were set in 1955 and, apart from the introduction of new materials, have changed little since then. The competition races require six boats, each with a four-man/women crew plus the all important sweep or coxswain, to launch from shallow water and go out through the surf for about 400m, turn around a buoy and row back to the beach. The winning crew are the first to cross the on-water finish line with any part of their boat, or alternatively one member of the crew may have to run and touch a flag on the beach.

post very interesting blogs, which give the reader a good insight into life on the ocean. They can give detailed descriptions of operating as a small team in a confined space, overcoming mechanical and technical failures or the mental toughness required to do it on your own. Records are being established that will no doubt be broken by the next generation of ocean rowers.

Challenge rowing has also included a variety of shorter events, such as crossing the English Channel, with Dover Rowing Club currently holding the record of 2hr 41min. Guin Batten, a silver medallist from the Sydney Olympics, has crossed the Channel in a fine sculling boat in four and a half hours. If you are interested in attempting any of these challenges, do research the rules first, as a pilot boat is

A team-building exercise.

A surfboat.

Indoor Rowing

Rowing machines, bank tubs and indoor rowing tanks have been around for a long time. The Gjessing-Nilsen machine was introduced in the 1970s as an accurate testing machine, but cost and the space required ensured it was mainly used for testing rather than training. In 1981, Concept 2 produced the first indoor rowing machine that could be made cheaply, transported easily and used in gyms, boat houses or homes. This established the indoor rowing machine as part of regular training for crews and as a sport in its own right. Now there is a range of machines available: both fixed-head and sliding-head ergometers. The ergometer cannot completely replicate the feeling of rowing on the water, but the coordination required, plus its ability to monitor outputs, make it a very effective training tool. There is a close correlation between people who go fast on the water and their ergometer scores, whilst the opposite is not necessarily true.

Indoor rowing is a popular sport in its own right, with many schools and gyms having their own banks of rowing machines. There are local, regional and national competitions for this type of rowing. Concept 2 still manufactures the most popular machines used for racing. A National Championships was held in Birmingham each year and a youth event is hosted in London by London Youth Rowing. There are many other local and regional events. The national events can cater for up to five thousand competitors, making this a mass participation event, with National and World Records often being set. A European Championships has recently been established. Many nations hold indoor rowing championships and Concept 2 hosts a 'World Event' in the USA each year, where the best from each nation compete.

Crew classes are also becoming popular, with many rowers participating together, as training on the rowing machine is a great way to get and stay fit. Classes are conducted by qualified instructors, often to music, with the workout varying depending on the make up of the class.

A Concept 2 rowing machine.

Table 5 Masters Rowing Categories

Masters category	Minimum years
A	27
B	36
C	43
D	50
E	55
F	60
G	65
H	70
I	75
J	80
K	85

Competitive Rowing

There will be races at different levels each weekend in the UK, which will either be processional or raced side by side. Every competitor should be able to find an event suitable for them, with a system categorizing the competitors into similar ability bands. There are also age bands for junior and masters competitors.

Racing Categories by Age Bands

Juniors The junior category is classified into age bands, arranging competitors into groups that are numbered one year higher than their birthday on 1 September each year. If they are 12 years old on 1 September, therefore, they will race in the J13 category. The age bands for juniors are: J9, J10, J11, J12, J13, J14, J15, J16, J17 and J18. The only racing categories for juniors, at J14 and below, are in sculling boats.

Under 23s A rower or coxswain can compete as under 23 until the year in which they reach their 22nd birthday by 31st December. The World Under 23s is an important event on the performance pathway, as there is a big correlation between those who excel at this level, and their ability to be successful as Senior and Olympic Rowers.

Masters Rowing The masters rowing category is organized in year bands. The status of the crew is defined by the average age of the crew. The age of the masters rower is calculated on the whole year they reach in the current calendar year. As the average age of the population increases (and depending on the age of entrants), additional age bands are added as necessary.

Lightweight Rowers

There are weight-restricted classes for the under 23 and senior categories. The international boat categories for men are LM1x, LM2x, LM4x, LM2-, LM4- and LM8+, with the double (2x) and four (4-) being Olympic classes. The international boat classes for women are LW1x, LW2x and LW4x, with only the double scull (2x) being an Olympic-class boat. Weights are set for both a crew average and as a maximum for any one rower. The averages are 70kg for men and 57kg for women, while the maximums are 72kg and 59kg respectively. The weight allowed for both male and female single scullers is the maximum level.

Para Rowing

Many athletes with disabilities row on a regular basis in clubs up and down the country. Many require no special equipment and take part in regular training and racing, while some will require specialist equipment, such as modified seats and handles. Para rowing or adaptive rowing races were first included at the Paralympic Games in 2008. There are currently six international boat classes, with four being recognized as Paralympic classes. These are a men's and women's arms and shoulders single scull, a mixed double trunk and arms and a mixed coxed four leg, trunk and arms. The other international boat classes are a mixed coxed four for rowers with an intellectual impairment and a mixed double scull for leg, trunk and arm rowers. The rowers are classified to place them into the racing categories.

There are an increasing number of programmes for para rowers within the UK and help is available to clubs to enable them to cater for a variety of disabilities. Racing opportunities exist and are continually being developed. The racing categories have recently been expanded and are likely to grow in the next few years.

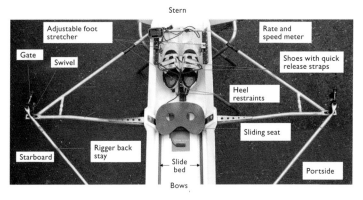

The named parts of a sculling boat.

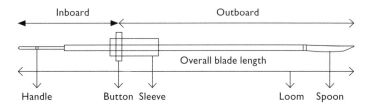

The parts of the blade.

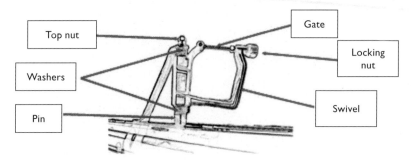

Types of rowlocks, thole pins and swivels.

each crew to have different blade lengths. The overall length of the blade can vary, as can the size of the spoon vary in terms of both length and width. The general principle is the smaller and slower the crew, the shorter the blade and smaller the spoon.

Coastal Boats and Fixed-Seat Boats

The terms used to identify the parts of these boats are universal and have been developed throughout the history of boatbuilding. The variations are in the construction, the number in the crew, the type of pins and rowlocks used to attach the blades to the boat, the variety of fixed and sliding seats, and whether the seating is offset or astern.

Lifting and Handling Equipment

Getting the Boat Off the Rack

Every boathouse will be different in layout but generally the boats are stored on racks one above the other upside down. Storing the boats on solid, level racks is important and supporting the boats at their bulkheads is critical to maintain the integrity of the boat. The crew should be able to lift a light racing boat off the rack. Care should be taken to avoid damaging either the boat you are moving or the boats below on the riggers that will extend below the gunwale of the boat. Rudders and fins are also prone to getting damaged when moving a boat from a rack and when launching it.

When lifting the boat from the rack, the crew should stand opposite their riggers and, as appropriate, one crew member or the cox will give instructions. Racing boats are not heavy but they are long and therefore the crew need to work together to carry the boat. In order to maximize storage space, boathouse bays are often fairly narrow, requiring the boat to be carried on the half turn when moving it out of the boathouse.

Carrying a Single Sculling Boat

There are several ways to carry a single sculling boat; either with the bottom or side resting on the shoulder and supported by the arm or upside down on the head. Whichever way you carry the boat the most important thing is to find the balance point and to practise lifting the boat. This is best tried from trestles in the first instance and then, once confident, from the rack.

Launching a Boat

Launching From a Bank

When launching on a river with a stream, boats should be launched with the bow pointing into the stream. This maximizes the steering ability of the single or crew whether using blades or a rudder to steer. This is particularly true when landing the boat, as the boat will move into the bank under rower power rather than being propelled by the wind or stream. On lakes the wind or position of the pontoons may determine the optimal direction for boating.

The named parts of a sculling boat.

Carrying the boat – 1.

Carrying the boat – 2.

Stored single sculling boats, showing how the boats need to be carefully lifted and rolled off the rack.

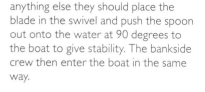

1.   Stepping on to the front stops and placing the blade into the waterside swivel, having already completed this for the bankside blade.

2.   Stepping onto the decking, holding the sculls in one hand and keeping the weight on the inside rigger.

3.   Sitting down and placing the feet into the shoes

front stops and they can then pull back horizontally on the handles as they lower themselves onto the seat.

Entering a Sweep Boat

The bankside crew place their blade into the swivel and hold the boat steady. The waterside crew place the blade across the boat near to the footboard. With the seat in the half-slide position, the rower can place one hand on each gunwale and place the waterside foot onto the front stops and then lower themselves down onto the seat. The rower should never stand in the bottom of the boat. Before they do

anything else they should place the blade in the swivel and push the spoon out onto the water at 90 degrees to the boat to give stability. The bankside crew then enter the boat in the same way.

Positioning the Foot Stretcher

Assuming that the equipment is set up correctly, then the foot stretcher should ensure that the relationship between the sculling handles or sweep blade to the body and hands is correct.

The Correct Position for Sculling

Assuming that the boat is rigged appropriately, then the rowers should move their feet to the correct position. To check their position they should sit at backstops with their legs down flat and the body leaning slightly back, as at the end of the drive phase. There should be one-and-a-half hand widths between the ends of the sculls when they are drawn in to the body, as at the finish of a stroke. The elbows should be above the hands and drawn backwards rather than outwards. If there is less than one-and-a-half hands between the scull handles, then move the foot stretcher towards the rower; if there is more than the required distance, move the foot stretcher towards the stern of the boat.

The Correct Position for Sweeping

The outside hand should be on the end of the handle and this should be in line with the outside of the body. The inside hand should be two hand widths further down the loom. The outside hand at the finish of the stroke with the layback and rotation should be outside the line of the body. The outside elbow should be drawn back behind the body

Sculling: when sitting at the finish position with the thumbs brushing the tee shirt, the hands should be one-and-a-half hand widths apart. This may become two hands widths apart when sculling with a lie back, but the hands are still inside the line of the body.

Sweeping: at the finish of the sweep stroke, the handle is level with the outside of the body and the outside hand can maintain pressure on the blade.

Spoon Shape

When the spoon is out of the water the difference in shape can be seen. The hydrodynamics around a blade are extremely complicated and a shape that may help you at one part of the stroke may hinder you in another. Prior to the introduction of the cleaver in 1991, nearly all rowing blades had the macon shape. This is still available and is excellent for young juniors or those learning the sport, since you have to learn how to lock the blade into the water, particularly at the catch.

There is now a range of spoon shapes, all derived from the big blade or cleaver. The cleaver or big blade spoon is shorter and fatter than the macon and the centre of pressure on the blade, so the point around which the blade turns is closer to the tip. This makes the load greater on the catch and the first third of the drive. There are variations on the shape, with a fat smoothie moving the centre of pressure closer to the tip of the spoon so it requires a shorter blade length. The spoon can also have a strip on the end called a vortex edge that moves the point of pressure closer to the end of the spoon. The fat smoothie and blades with

a vortex edge have the feeling of the heaviest load on the catch and the big blade or cleaver have the least. The overall length of the fat smoothie blade is about 5–10cm shorter than a big blade, slick or smoothie. Your choice is a personal one and depends on your technique and power profile. The manufacturer's websites give good information on what equipment is most suitable for a range of crews.

Shaft Stiffness, Weight and Overall Length

Shafts can be made wholly of carbon fibre or with other composite materials included, or they can be made of wood. A carbon shaft will be lighter and the materials can be arranged in different ways to change its stiffness. Generally the rule is that the stronger the crew, or the faster the boat, then the stiffer the shaft should be. So an elite men's eight may use a stiff shaft while a J14 girl's quad may use softer shafts. There are different weights of blades and the very light ones require a higher level of skill to control in windy conditions and they tend not to be so robust. The

manufacturers give good guidance on which blades are appropriate for different uses.

Rigging the Boat

In order to accommodate a variety of rowers, nearly everything in the cockpit area can be adjusted. The seats come in a variety of heights, the shoes sizes available reflect the range of rowers, and the angle, height and position of the feet can all be changed. The width and height of the rigger plus the pitch on the blade and swivel can all be adjusted. Be very clear about how you want your crew to row and then rig the boat to enable this to happen.

There is a sequence that, if followed, makes rigging the boat effective. A plan for rigging a boat should consider the interaction of different measurements and whether any variation to the normal rigging sequence may need to be considered.

Find a clear piece of ground and place the boat the right way up on trestles. The more horizontal this is the better, but it is not essential. Even a small boat will take an hour to rig, so

The variety of big blade types.

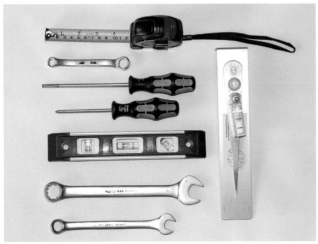

The tools required to rig a boat.

Span and Spread

The span or spread is the first measurement to be set. The right span or spread will enable the crew to get the required length of stroke if combined with the right blade inboard. Span is used for sculling boats and spread for sweep boats. Spread is measured from the middle of the boat to the middle of the bottom of the pin. Try to keep the tape measure as straight as possible.

The span is measured between the middle of the bottom of the pins. Check that the pins are the same distance from the midline of the boat by measuring from the slide to the top of the opposite pin and check this is the same measure on both sides of the boat. The slides should be set equidistant from the midline of the boat.

find a place where you will not have to keep moving the boat. Secure the boat with supports under the riggers to ensure it is not moving from side to side. Try to level the boat using a spirit level when putting these in place.

Centre of Work and Midline of the Boat

Before starting to rig the boat mark the centre of work and the middle of the boat. The centre of work is a line from the base of the pin and at 90 degrees to the midline of the boat. Some manufacturers put a line in the cockpit showing the centre of work but if you move the rigger position this will no longer be in the correct place.

The midline of the boat comes from the middle of the bows to the middle of the stern. It can be easily found for each seat by measuring the width of the cockpit and halving it.

Measuring the spread.

Measuring the span.

Ensuring that both pins are equidistant from the midline of the boat.

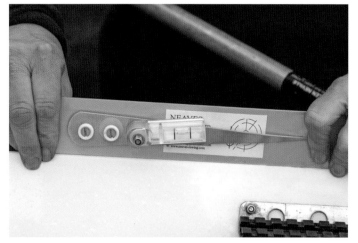

LEFT: Setting the pitch meter to zero in the bow-to-stern direction.

BOTTOM LEFT: Measuring the stern pitch on the pin.

BOTTOM: Changing the pin pitch.

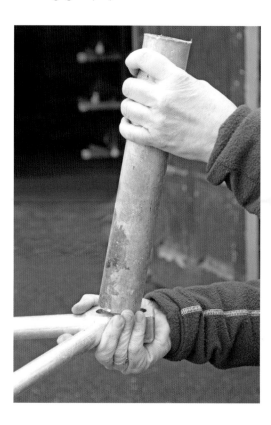

Stern Pitch

Correct pitch will enable the blade to 'sit' in the correct position in the water. In order to catch the water, the rower must lift the blade handle, and a small amount of pitch on the swivel will stop the blade from going too deep at the catch. To set the pitch, remove the swivel from the pin and set this to one side with the washers. The pitch should be zeroed in the stern–bow direction. Most pitch meters enable you to set up the meter to accommodate the boat on even ground. Ensure the pitch meter is placed on a level surface in the boat such as the keel of the boat or on the decking, providing the deck does not slope (most single sculling boats have a sloping decking). Zero the pitch meter and then hold it hard against the pin and read the gauge.

Many riggers do not have adjustable pitch but new boats arrive with the pitch on zero. The pitch can change when the blades get caught in the water or if the riggers get knocked. In order to return the pitch to zero, use a long hollow tube. Place this over the pin and gently pull the pin into the desired position. When doing this, try to isolate the action to the pin and ensure the rigger is supported and that there is no excessive force put on the boat.

Lateral Pitch

Lateral pitch is added to the pin in order to change the angle of the blade through the stroke. One and a half degrees of lateral pitch adds about 1 degree of pitch at the catch to 5 degrees. In the middle of the stroke, the pitch will still be 4 degrees, and at the finish about 3 degrees. This small adjustment further stops the blade from going deep on the catch, maximizes the spoon area locked into the water in the middle of the stroke and assists extraction of the blade at the finish of the stroke. Lateral pitch can vary from 0 to 1.5 degrees with the pin leaning out from the midline of the boat. The boat must be level from portside to starboard. Use a spirit level and set the pitch meter to zero on top of this. Hold the pitch meter securely against the pin and at 90 degrees to the boat. Any adjustments need to be made as above.

Swivel Inserts

Most swivels come with a series of inserts that enable the pitch on the swivel to be set between 1 and 7 degrees. The most usual pitch is 4 degrees. The more competent the crew, the less overall pitch will be required.

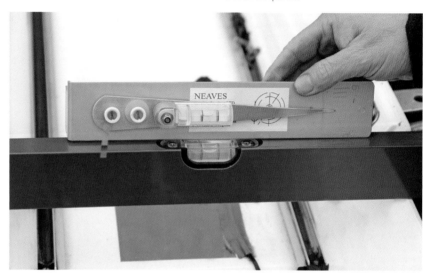

Setting the pitch meter to zero for later pitch measurement.

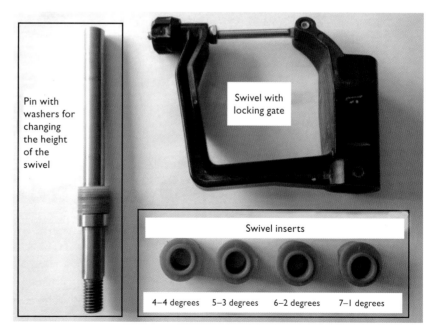

Pin with washers for changing the height of the swivel

Swivel with locking gate

Swivel inserts

4–4 degrees   5–3 degrees   6–2 degrees   7–1 degrees

Swivel inserts.

Setting the height stick a third of the way down the sill of the swivel.

Height of work from seat to swivel sill

Measuring the height of work using a height stick.

Move washers under/on top of the swivel to adjust the height of work.

Swivel Height

The height of the swivel is important. Too high and the rower will struggle to get the blade into the water; too low and the rower will not be able to use the upper body correctly (there will be little room for error or ability to cope with rough conditions). There is an articulated parallelogram that can be used to measure height. The parallelogram is placed across the saxboards and carefully opened so the long end is placed one third of the way down the sill of the swivel. The height is the distance from the seat up to the bottom of the top bar. Heights can be adjusted by putting more or fewer washers below the swivel.

Heights should be in the range of 15–19cm for sculling boats and 16–19cm for sweep boats. The lowest heights will be recommended for the smallest rowers, so the lightweight women's category, and the highest for open weight men. Rowers with long bodies may need more height. If the crew is rowing in too large a boat then the height can be lowered but 14–16cm is usually the minimum or there is not enough room to control the blade on the recovery.

Feet Height

The correct height of the feet below the seat will enable the rower to get their shins vertical. If the feet are too low there will be a tendency to over compress or, more likely, for the body to fall over the thighs and open in the first part of the drive. If the feet are too high, the rower may struggle to get their hips over from the finish and the stroke may be completely reliant on the legs, with little body involvement. The feet height below the seat is measured from the saxboard down to the seat and then the saxboard down to the bottom of the feet:

Feet below saxboard − seat below saxboard = feet below seat.

The range for this measurement is

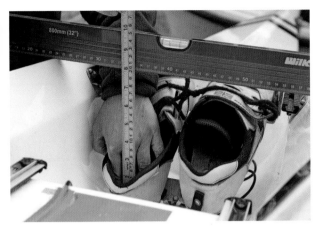

Measuring the feet height below the saxboard/gunwale.

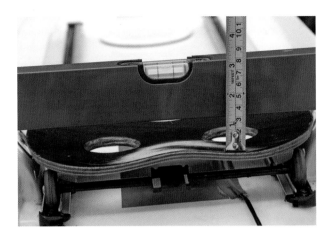

Measuring the seat height below the saxboard/gunwale.

16–19cm, and for those with really large feet, it may be 20cm if room in the boat permits.

Stretcher Angle

The feet height and angle are inter-related in terms of enabling the rower to get into the right position. The optimal angle from the horizontal for the stretcher angle is 42 degrees, with a range of 40–45 degrees. Rowers who are very flexible, including young rowers, may be inclined to over compress and so a steeper stretcher angle of 45 degrees will help to stop this. Rowers who are inflexible or who have stiff ankles will find a flatter angle helpful as it enables them to get full compression. If this is an issue, rowers should work on flexibility. Coaches need to ensure the rower does not fall over their knees and open the body too early in the drive. The relative length of the thigh and shin will also impact on the correct setting for the angle and height of the feet.

Setting the Catch and Finish Angles

The sculling and sweep angles are given in the next chapter. However, it is very helpful if a marker can help the rower to reach the required angles. A mark on the boat for where the handle needs to come to and similarly a straw at front stops can help the rower reach the required angles on the catch.

Putting Straws on the Boat

Giving a physical marker for a crew can help them all to row to the right length. Usually straws are used, as they will remain in a vertical position when attached to the side of the boat. They will also not injure the rower if they are touched with the hand or arm. Tables exist (see Appendix 2) that use trigonometry to work out where the straws need to be placed for any required angle. The tables are organized with span or spread and the required angles. Place a string line down the centre of the boat

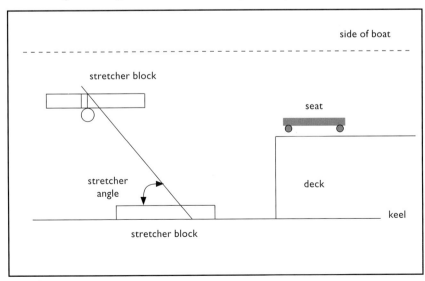

The stretcher angle.

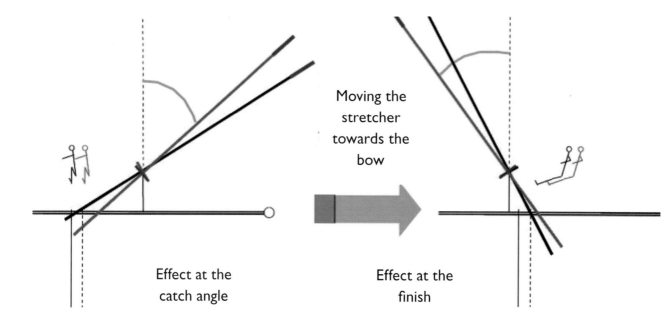

Moving the stretcher towards the bow

Effect at the catch angle

Effect at the finish

The effects of adjusting the foot stretcher on catch and finish angles.

from the bows to the stern. Decide what angle you require and use the tables to look up the distance in cm that this must be from the base of the pin to the centre line of the boat. Where the tape measure meets the mid-point of the boat is the required angle. Straws can be placed where the tape measure passes over the side on the boat. Add these by placing a metal bar in the swivel and attaching it firmly to the face of the swivel using an elastic band.

Setting Inboard and Outboard on the Blade

Modern blades are adjustable in total length and inboard length or outboard length (see Appendix 2 for recommended blade lengths). The blade length should be measured to the tip of the spoon in line with the shaft. The inboard is measured from the button (which presses against the swivel when rowing) to the end of the handle.

Overlap

The blades in sculling overlap during the midpoint of the stroke and the sweep handle extends over the midline of the boat. Span and spread are measured to the middle of the pin but when calculating

BELOW TOP: Measuring overall blade length.

BELOW BOTTOM: Measuring inboard blade length.

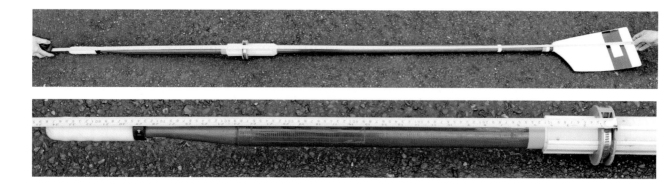

TOP: *Measuring outboard blade length.*

LEFT: *Measuring the length of the spoon.*

RIGHT: *Measuring the width of the spoon at its widest point.*

the overlap half of the width of the swivel has to be taken into account. (*See Appendix 2 for calculations.*)

Rigger Position

The position of the pin in relation to the stern and bows will already have

been determined by the boatbuilder. Some boats give a range of stern/bow rigger positions. Bringing the rigger positions closer to the middle of the boat can help straight line speed, especially in pairs. The rigger position can affect the trim of the boat. This position should enable the rower to get the length of stroke with the arc in the

right ratio. In fixed-seat boats everything tends to be fixed, so changing the rigger or pin position is not usually an option.

Specialized Equipment

Rowing is a very inclusive sport that can cater for a wide range of disabilities. Many people will not need any modifications to equipment but a few will need modifications or even specialized equipment. British Rowing has a good resource that can help with information on catering for a range of abilities. Of the three Paralympic Classifications, the 'Arms and Shoulders' para-rowers require a suitable boat with floats and a modified rig with a narrow span and short blades. The 'Trunk and Arms' rowers require modified equipment and a suitable rig. For these two categories of rower the boats are shorter, wider and more stable than river-racing boats. The 'Leg, Trunk and Arms' rowers use a racing coxed four, but depending on their disability, may need modified equipment such as blade handles or foot stretchers.

Ergometers

There are a whole variety of ergometers

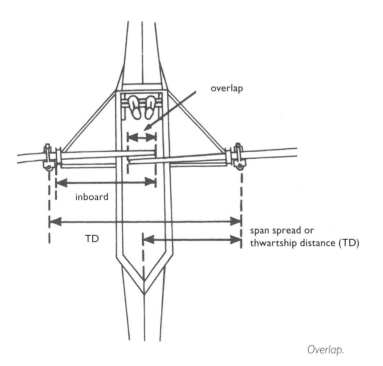

overlap

inboard

TD

span spread or
thwartship distance (TD)

Overlap.

Paralympic and World Champion in the Men's AS category, Tom Agar rowing in a boat with a Paralympic seat and strapping.

A Concept 2 fixed-head rowing machine and an Oartec Slider.

on sale but the most popular for rowing clubs and gyms in the UK is the Concept 2. The Concept 2, Row Perfect and Oartec use air that drives a fan for resistance and the feel of the rowing can be changed by altering the air flow and hence the drag on the flywheel. As these machines are regulated by airflow then setting them up by measuring the drag is a good way to ensure they always feel the same, no matter what the air temperature or humidity. The manual will show you how to achieve this simple set up. The Water Rower derives the resistance by using a paddle in a water tank. Variations in feel can be achieved by changing the level of water in the tank. The final major variation in ergometer design is the fixed-head or moving-head ergometer.

Row Perfect, the Oartech and Concept all produce a sliding-head ergometer and the standard Concept 2 can be placed on sliders to make it feel more like a sliding-head ergometer. The advantage of the sliders is that the machines can be linked to each other and so the whole crew must learn to move together. The difference between the fixed-head and sliding-head ergometers is the feel, mainly at the catch, and a few studies have also shown that the technique can vary. The fixed-head ergometer encourages early opening of the body and a longer stroke, particularly at the finish, while the sliding-head ergometer requires greater coordination at the catch with the leg drive and body stability and it produces a shorter stroke.

All of these ergometers are robust machines and, just as when choosing a boat, you should try it out first, particularly if it is for training and keeping fit rather than entering competitions. At the current time, most competitions take place on the Concept 2 or the Water Rower.

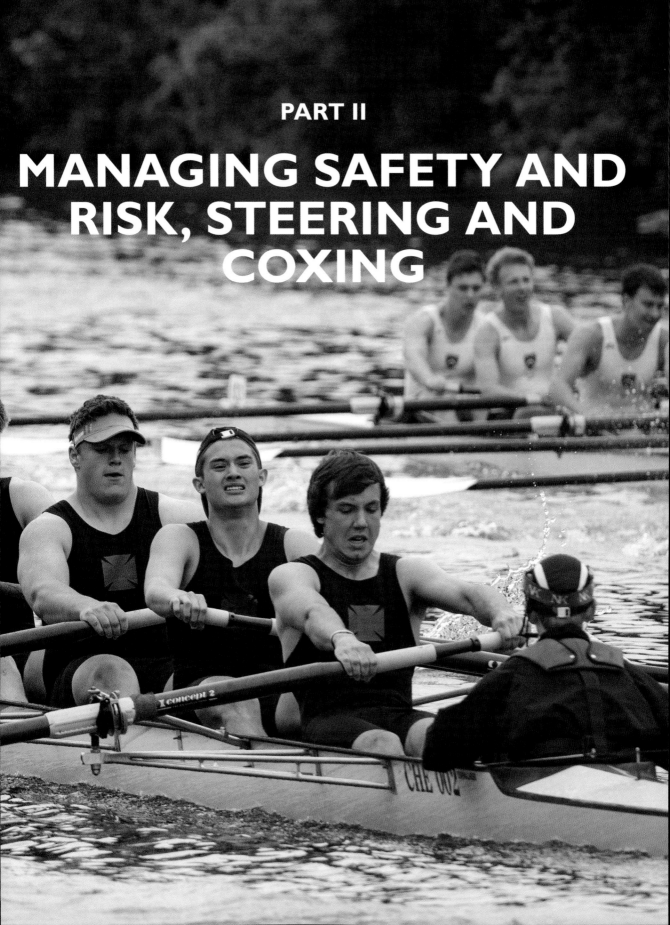

PART II

MANAGING SAFETY AND RISK, STEERING AND COXING

For example, have an attempt at towing the boat the wrong way up while it is still capsized. Generally there is more drag on the boat and you will move more slowly, but this may still be quicker than righting the boat if you fall in near the bank.

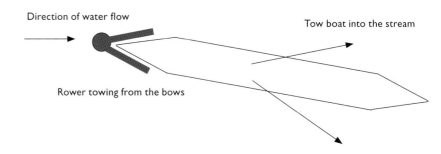

Direction of water flow

Tow boat into the stream

Rower towing from the bows

Towing a boat into the stream.

Towing

If you are towing a boat and there is any stream or wind, then you should tow against the stream or into the head wind. You can then see where you are drifting and any obstacles or hazards that you might be about to hit. The boat will hit any obstacle before you do and you can therefore take avoiding action.

Towing is not always an option if the conditions are unfavourable, with low water temperatures, high winds or a fast stream or tide, for example, or if the distance from the bank is too great. The boat may be too heavy and big to tow, and in these instances staying with the boat and getting as much of your body out of the water as possible is the best option. Try climbing onto the upturned hull by using the same technique as used for getting back into the boat in deep water (see later in this section). Be aware of the weather conditions, as cold water affects your muscles and your ability to swim. Even the best swimmers can be unable to swim in cold conditions when

their muscles fail to work (also known as swim failure). Once on the hull, try paddling the boat using your hands and legs.

Re-entering the Boat from Deep Water

Try getting back into the boat from the water when the boat is the right way up. There are two ways to attempt this: over the bow of the boat or at the rigger. If you elect to come over the bow then you need to sit astride the bow canvas and make your way along this, keeping your centre of gravity as low as possible. If possible, tie the scull handles together to provide lateral stability on the boat. Once you get to the cockpit, you will need to

bring the scull handles together or grasp the handles and then swing your legs into the boat. You should then be in a position to continue to scull your boat. If you elect to come into the boat near the rigger then you need to grasp hold of both scull handles in one hand and raise your body over the side of the boat so you are lying across the boat and over the slide beds. Use a strong leg kick to raise your body out of the water. You will need to get your hips above the saxboard and then you can swing your legs into the boat and once again continue to scull back to the boathouse.

Entering from Shallow Water and Landing

Beware of obstructions and underwater objects, vegetation or soft mud and glass. Try to empty as much water as possible from the boat by tipping it before getting back into it.

Using the 'Buddy' System of Rescue

One way of rescuing an individual in the water using your own single scull is to get them to support themselves on your stern deck. The individual can then be supported out of the water, which should reduce the amount of time they are immersed and losing body heat rapidly. You may be still able to scull the boat to safety or call for help.

Climbing onto the upturned hull.

Climbing back into the boat from the side.

Buddy rescue.

Rules for Staying Safe

Stay with the boat at all times.

- A capsized or swamped boat provides you with a buoyant raft.
- A capsized boat is more easily seen by those coming to help than just a head in the water.
- You should pull your body out of the water and onto the hull to reduce rapid cooling.
- Re-enter the boat if the conditions allow.
- Keeping the whole crew together enables you to help each other and to be more visible.
- Only leave your boat when you know you are safe or that staying with the boat will take you into greater danger (for example, if the boat no longer constitutes an effective life raft).

Rowing offers a huge range of boat types, challenges and races as well as the opportunity to just mess about on the river. As a non-weight bearing activity it is suitable for a wide range of ages, sizes and abilities. Whatever you decide to do on the water, ensure that you always conduct a risk assessment and keep yourself and other water users safe. Now it is time to choose and set up your equipment so you can get going.

CHAPTER 5

STEERING, COXING AND COMMANDS

Steering

A proficient steersperson is always welcome in a boat because their ability can make rowing easier for the crew. The good cox or crew steersperson has outstanding watermanship skills and authority. A good waterman understands how the water, environmental conditions, boat and crew will interact and can respond accordingly to any situation. Authority ensures the crew respond to the commands issued by the steersperson. Steering the boat in the least intrusive way for the crew is essential as this will help with balance and timing and ensure the boat travels in the most efficient way – generally a straight line.

The Role of the Cox

Usually all boats have a steering mechanism, apart from single and double sculls, but all will need to be manoeuvred and steered. Many boats have a coxswain and the role they play is vital since as well as making the rowing easy for the crew they are responsible for the safety of the crew, equipment and other water users. Undertaking a risk assessment before each session and monitoring the situation constantly is a critical element of their duties. The role of the cox starts before the outing to ensure all the equipment is in good working order. It is their responsibility to ensure that the rudder is working and properly fitted to the boat. The cox will control the boat from the time the crew launch until all the equipment is returned to its original storage position. Once they have acquired steering skills and coxing commands then a good cox will be able to get the best from the crew whatever their status or level of experience. They anticipate actions required to improve the rowing such as rhythm, timing, work rate or technical calls. The right call will bring a crew together, improve their boat speed and motivate them to work more effectively. The right call at the right time will also create trust between cox and crew. Feedback from the coach and crew can enable the cox to improve their responses in a variety of situations.

If you are going to be taking on this role and are going onto a new piece of water for the first time, make sure you know the local rules and what the potential hazards are on that stretch. Ask for expert advice and usually any of the groups with responsibility for the water will be pleased to give advice about local rules and navigation.

Within the UK, a racing crew can be steered by a male or female cox. For FISA-regulated international racing events the gender of the cox must be the same as that of the crew, otherwise gender rules can vary between countries.

Position in the Boat

The coxswain should ensure their weight is in the middle of the boat and should remain as still as possible throughout the outing. In a stern-coxed boat, their feet may need to brace against the bulkhead to stop them moving backwards and forwards excessively during the stroke cycle. This is equally important in a bow-coxed boat, which is a racing pair (or four or quad). Placing the cox in the bows reduces the length of the boat, gets the cox's weight low down in the boat and redistributes the weight of the crew, which enables the boat to run more efficiently. A bow-steered boat enables the cox to have a clear view of where they are going. The disadvantage is they cannot see the crew or any boat coming from behind, so this option is only suitable for an experienced cox. In a stern-coxed boat the cox can see the crew but their view immediately in front of the boat is obstructed. Ideally the cox should keep their weight as low as possible in the boat but this compounds the situation. When coxing a boat, be prepared to ask the bow or stroke to assist you if your view is obstructed, especially on unfamiliar water, when manoeuvring or when there are lots of other boats on the water.

The Steersperson

The steersperson gives the commands in the boat and this often includes calls during training and racing. On a river the

Table 7   Cox's Weight Categories in the UK

Racing Category	Weight (kg)	Dead weight
Men: Senior, masters, J18, J17, J16 mixed crews	55	The dead weight is ideally one item and if using sand or liquid it must be in a sealed unit.
Women: Senior, masters, WJ18, WJ17, WJ16	50	
J15 and WJ15 crews and younger		

steersperson is most likely to be in the bows of the boat as they have the best view in the direction of travel. Their voice can be easily heard by the crew. On a multi-lane course the steersperson maybe in the stern of the boat since the steering is taken from the buoys and the view behind the boat. In this situation the racing and training calls may need to be made by a person nearer to the bows of the boat.

Rudders

Generally the slower and bigger the boat, the larger the rudder. For an Olympic rowing eight the rudder is behind the fin to minimize drag. The rudder may be very small but once applied at racing speeds it can move the boat very effectively. At slow speeds or when backing the boat down (manoeuvring the boat backwards) then the rudder will have minimal effect.

Rudder Lines

The rudder wires or rope should be securely attached to the rudder and able to move freely. In modern racing boats the rudder lines can be under the stern canvas. A stern-coxed boat should have the rudder lines uncrossed. In a coxless or bow-steered boat the lines will pass by a series of rowers to reach the steersperson's shoes or the cox's rudder lever. The rudder lines must move freely and cross over whether they are on top of or under the stern canvas.

   The rudder lines should remain taut at all times. Any slack in the lines will delay the application of the rudder and hence delay the change of boat direction. When using a steering foot the rudder lines should be adjusted for different stretcher settings. For the stern-coxed boat there are toggles attached to the line that can be moved to enable the cox to be in the most comfortable and stable position.

   If using a steering foot or rudder lines then the steersperson or cox should know exactly when the rudder is straight. The shoe fixing to the rudder wire can be

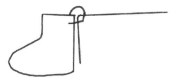

A large stern rudder generally to be found on slow moving boats such as coastal boats

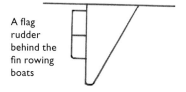

A flag rudder behind the fin rowing boats

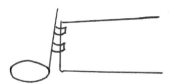

A stern rudder such as the ones on Explore rowing boats

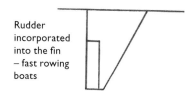

Rudder incorporated into the fin – fast rowing boats

Types of rudders.

moved slightly to accommodate different feet positions.

How the Rudder Works

When the boat has forward momentum then applying the rudder will make the boat turn. The rudder works by deflecting water and changing the drag on the boat. The stern of the boat moves to the side with least drag. The bows keep in the same place and the stern swings round, which is why applying the rudder slows the boat down so much. A fine boat rolls slightly to the side to which it is moving, so making the boat unstable for the crew to row.

   When backing the boat down the rudder should be held straight by the cox or steersperson. If not then it is likely to get caught by the water and pushed to an extreme position that will cause it to act as a break and this may steer the boat in the wrong direction. After such an incident getting the rudder straight can sometimes be difficult.

   In order to move to port side then the stern-seated cox pushes their right hand or portside hand forward. For the

steersperson they point their toe to portside and the bow cox points the rudder lever to portside. The reverse is true to move to starboard.

When to Steer

Ideally the rudder should be applied when the blades are in the water so as to minimize the balance issues for the crew. This means the rudder is far less effective in turning the boat. The steersperson/cox should anticipate steering requirements and apply the rudder early in small pulses while the blades are in the water. There is a delay between applying the rudder and any perceived movement of the boat since the stern is skidding sideways. The inexperienced steersperson/cox can underestimate the amount the boat will turn and this can mean they are constantly applying the rudder to try to keep to a straight line.

Steering with the Blades

The steersperson/cox can ask the crew to use their blades to assist steering the boat. This is especially helpful when turning the boat through 180 degrees, on a tight bend, at a buoy turn or when the bows rather than the stern should move. In singles and doubles there is no rudder and all the steering is from the blades. This is achieved by pulling on portside blades to go to starboard and vice versa. For small steering adjustments the focus should be on pushing harder on the foot stretcher on the side requiring extra power. So if you wish to steer to starboard then push harder with portside or right foot. The most effective point of the stroke for steering with the blades is at the catch, so sharpening slightly with one side or delaying the catch on one side can also help to steer the boat.

Forward Momentum

The rudder only works when there is forward momentum on the boat. This is why launching from and returning to the dock into the stream means that even at low speeds the rudder will work. Coming into the bank with a strong stream leaves little possibility of the rudder working; not only will the rudder be very ineffective but the blades are also less effective when travelling against the stream.

Stopping the boat

Ensure that the crew practise stopping the boat both from slow speeds and full race pace. This skill should be practised at regular intervals, particularly when a new crew combination is formed. Not only may stopping the boat quickly prevent a collision, it may also be used to pick up an ejected crew member. (There is a possibility that a crew member could be ejected from the boat by catching their blade on an obstacle or getting the blade caught into the water.) Stopping the boat quickly and continually spotting where the crew member is in the water is critical, particularly in rough or flowing water.

Steering Hints

Use the conditions and environment to your best advantage. This can include using the stream or wind to control the boat by maintaining position or to turn the boat. By keeping the bows facing into the stream or wind it makes it easier to maintain position because the crew can take small adjusting strokes. Putting the bows out into a stream while keeping the stern out of the stream will help to turn the boat. If there is no stream but a wind this can be similarly used.

Steering in a Stream

When rowing on moving water such as a river or tidal body of water there are considerations for enabling the sculler or crew to be most efficient. If rowing with the stream then try to maintain a position with both sides of the boat rowing in water moving at a similar speed If this is not possible then put the bows of the boat into the slightly faster-moving water. This will ensure the side of the boat out of the stream is not having to continually work harder to keep the boat straight. When going against the stream, such as rowing on a fast-moving river, then the bow should be kept very slightly facing into the bank. If it is not then the bows will be caught by the stream and the blades in the stream will be working harder continually to keep the boat straight.

Bridges, Moored Boats, Standing Waves, Weirs

Turn downstream of any obstacles so the boat cannot be swept onto them. Weirs can potentially create a serious hazard if not respected. Turn well above them and know which conditions require changes to normal practice.

Communication

Any steersperson/cox must be able to

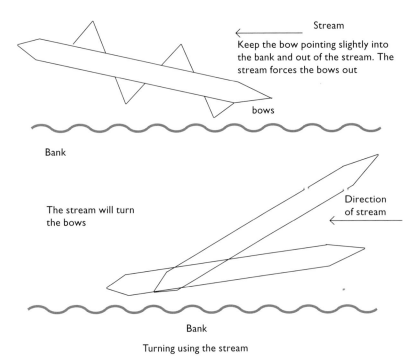

Stream

Keep the bow pointing slightly into the bank and out of the stream. The stream forces the bows out

bows

Bank

The stream will turn the bows

Direction of stream

Bank

Turning using the stream

Steering in a stream.

communicate effectively and needs to know the commands to use with the crew. In the early stages a cox may be limited to the coxing commands but later calls to assist the crew to row more efficiently should be added. There should be a systematic development of the ability of the cox to add value to the rowing. Feedback from the crew will assist the cox to develop the right calls and coaching points to improve rowing efficiency.

Coaching the Cox or Steersperson

A good starting point would be to share the risk assessment for their home reach. This will ensure a discussion has taken place about the hazards on the stretch of water. This can include the hazards presented in different conditions and steering around obstacles such as bridges. A variety of experiences should be set for the cox or steersperson so they can build their confidence gradually. A checklist can ensure the training is complete. This may include areas such as coxing a bow- or stern-coxed boat or steering a variety of boat types.

The competences can be developed gradually to include steering on an unfamiliar piece of water or in a race both side by side and processional. This may involve getting onto a stake boat or maintaining the position of the boat while waiting to start as head of the river race, for example.

In the same way that a good rower can feel the boat, so can a good cox. Matching the coaching points to the feel of the boat is important, as are looking at the speed meter and seeing what the rhythm feels like at higher boat speeds. If possible being outside the crew on a bike or in a launch can help the cox to interpret their view from the cox's seat. They can then start to match their view to crew and individual coaching calls and intervene appropriately.

Coxing and steering are part of watermanship and this vital skill should be learned by all rowers. A crew with rowers who can all single scull, steer and/or cox is usually far more responsive to coxing commands, racing calls and coaching.

The Inexperienced Crew

An inexperienced crew should have an experienced cox to ensure they are safe, given appropriate instructions and do not cause problems for other water users. An inexperienced cox will learn the art of watermanship more quickly when a member of an experienced crew takes responsibility for the crew and cox. They are able to instruct the cox and once the cox is slightly more experienced they can share insights into technical issues such as rhythm and technical faults.

Coxing Commands

The primary role of the cox is the safety of the crew, the equipment and other water users. The cox must have authority in the boat and they issue commands that must be acted upon by the whole crew. If the crew act as a unit then carrying and launching the boat, on-water manoeuvring and rowing will be safer and easier. For the purposes of this section we refer to 'coxing orders' but this could equally be the crew member designated to give orders in the boat.

At the Boathouse
When taking the boat from the rack and out of the boathouse commands might include:

- **'Hands on'** This refers to the crew standing in an appropriate place to lift the boat, usually from a rack or trailer.
- **'Are you ready?'**
- **'Lift'** This is to ensure the whole crew lift the boat together.
- **'Roll the boat off the rack'** Usually the rack positions mean the boats need to be rolled off the rack to miss the riggers on boats above and below.

- If all the rowers are on the same side of the boat then an order should be given for **'Starboard side hold the boat portside under'**. The crew should be organized to be opposite their rigger when the boat is keel-side-up or beside their rigger when the right way up.
- **'Half turn'** This is for carrying the boat through tight spaces so is often used coming into and out of the boathouse where the aisle space is limited. The cox or crew leader will say which side riggers need to be up. So **'Half turn starboard riggers up'** would be the whole command. When rolling the boat off the rack it is obvious which side riggers need to be up but it is less obvious when returning to the boathouse or squeezing through a restricted space.
- **'Level'** This refers to carrying the boat keel-side-up at arm's length, so generally from a half-turn position.
- **'Up to shoulders lift'** This refers to carrying the boat on the shoulders of the crew.
- **'Down to waists go'** This would be used when taking the boat back to being carried at arm's length by the rowers' side.

There may be a need to turn the boat around to ensure the bows are pointing into the stream. The cox will need to be very clear about which way they want the crew to turn: **'Bows to the water, starboard side moving upstream'**. There will be local ways of achieving this so ensure the whole crew leader is aware of this and has communicated effectively with the crew. This will be said in many and varying ways but the cox must always be clear and concise.

Launching the Boat
In order to get a fine boat onto the water the crew all need to be standing on the same side of the boat. This can be achieved in several different ways depending on the experience of the crew and the weight of the boat. With a heavy boat or less experienced crew then the boat is rolled over and all the

crew hold a fixed part inside the boat (so not the foot stretcher or seat but possibly a strut or bar across the inside of the boat). The cox can then instruct the rowers to come under the boat or around the boat one by one until they all stand the on the same side. They need to reach across sufficiently inside the boat so the boat remains reasonably level.

A more experienced crew may chose to throw the boat above their heads and then the waterside people would move to the bankside. All must find a firm holding place in the boat as the boat moves above them and they then swing the boat down to waist level. A fine boat is very light so this is very easy to achieve but it needs a little experience and confidence to make it work.

'Above heads go' is a command for throwing the boat above head height so the side nearest the water can move under the boat away from the water's edge. Depending on the launch place the cox may ask the crew to wade into the water or feel for the edge of the pontoon with their foot, using the commands 'walk forward together', 'feel for the edge of the pontoon' and 'lower together'.

Boarding the Boat
'Starboard hold the boat: portside collect their blades'
would be used when, with the boat on the water, the portside swivels and blades are closest to the bank. Portside will collect their blades, place them in the swivels and hold on to the boat or the rigger. (Note: do not be tempted to stand on the rigger to hold the boat as they can easily be damaged and this can change the rigging including the pitch, which can make rowing difficult.) The starboard rowers should then collect their blades and place them across the boat and on command (**'one foot in – in'**) step into the boat, being careful about where they place their feet. They should then sit down and place their blade into the swivel and push out onto the water.

Generally that side of the boat adjust and then the cox will instruct the starboard side of the boat to step in together. If boarding from a pontoon once both sides are ready to row then the cox can get into the boat and ask the crew to **'push off together'**. Again, depending on the location and circumstance, this will vary. Off a stage this might be **'one hand on the stage'** and, once all the hands are there, **'push off'**. If wading into a river then the bow person might step into the boat last with the cox and push off with the cox as they do so. Find out what works locally and ensure the cox is safe, clear and concise with their commands. Quite often a **'go'** is added to the command so that there is a very clear time to move together.

For sculling boats the cox will use a variation of asking the crew to collect their blades and place them in the boat and also dictate the order of getting the crew in the boat. With sculling blades both blades can be placed into the swivel and used by the crew to step into the boat together. They can even push off the dock together and then sit down.

Surf boats and coastal boats are usually launched into the sea bow first. The blades are generally put into the boat before it is launched. This can mean that the sea is up to the rowers' waist or higher before they get into the boat. Often the bow rowers are boated first so they can very quickly row to control the position of the boat and to stop it being beached or turning broadside onto the waves.

Getting Ready to Row
Once the crew is ready to row then the cox or crew leader, who is often the bow steersperson, will call the commands. The first command will be for the crew to adjust their feet to the right position. Feet height may also need to be adjusted. In order to ensure that each member of crew is ready to row the cox will ask the crew to **'number off from bow when ready'**. Once this is completed then the

crew will be asked to **'Come forward. Light Paddle. Are you ready? Go'**. All the commands come from the cox and will include pressure changes, manoeuvres and any emergency safety issues.

In order for the crew to respond to a command it is best if the cox gives any call over three strokes. An example of this might be for changing the pressure – **'Next stroke. Paddle firm. Go'** – with the orders given over three strokes and the pressure change to come on the third stroke.

Stopping the Boat
Being able to stop the boat effectively is vitally important and the usual order for stopping the crew rowing together is 'easy all'. **'Easy'** is given as the blade goes into the water and **'all'** as the blade comes out. The stopping position is the safe position with the handles on the saxboard. On command the whole crew can 'drop' the blades flat onto the water. The crew should be able to stop in an emergency. The order will be **'hold her all'** and the flat blades will be slapped onto the water. **'Hold her hard'** would be for the blades to be slapped and buried and then reversed in the water as for backing down.

Turning the Boat
The boat can be turned by a variety of methods and the one chosen depends on the situation. The easiest is to have one side rowing on and the other sitting with their blades flat on the water. This is slow, however, and will take the boat in a very wide loop so is not effective for many stretches of water. To speed this up the cox can command the other side of the boat to **'hold the boat'**. A spin turn will require both sides to move together, with one side rowing on and the other backing down on the appropriate part of the stroke. The side called backs first so the whole crew start from backstops. **'Portside spin'** is the order.

Manoeuvring
Manoeuvring the boat can be achieved

by asking one rower or a side to **'touch her once'**. This can be changed to apply to more strokes if needed. Once on a stake boat (anchored boat used as a starting point) or if the boat needs to move sideways rather than around then the order can be given for **'two row with bows blade'**. This is very effective at moving the boat sideways.

Coming Alongside

At the end of the session the boat should be brought into the bank with bows into the wind or stream. This maximizes the steering at very low speeds. The bows come in at an angle and then by applying the rudder the stern of the boat will swing round towards the bank. The cox must ensure the riggers and blades are feathered high above the landing stage; the crew may need to lean slightly onto the waterside blades to make this happen.

Getting Out and Lifting Out

Once alongside the boarding procedures are reverse: **'Starboard side out. Hold the riggers'**. Portside then take out their blades and lay them across the boat and the order is given for **'portside out'**. The portside take their blades to the side of the stage. Orders are then given for taking the boat out of the water: **'Hands on. Are you ready? Lift'**. The crew need to be careful to ensure the rudder and fin as well as the riggers are not damaged at this time. Once the boat is out of the water then the orders for moving half the crew under the boat or throwing the boat over to get the crew spread on each side of it are essential. The instructions are then given to get the boat back onto trestles to be wiped down before being returned to the boathouse.

Ensure the boat is facing the right direction to go back into the boathouse; the boat will usually be carried into the boat house on the half turn. Ensure the appropriate riggers are up to enable the crew to roll the boat back onto the rack. **'Hold her port, under starboard'** will be the order and crew members may well need to reach across the boat to keep the inside riggers up as they return it to the rack.

Coming alongside – 1.

Coming alongside – 2.

PART III

SKILLS AND TECHNIQUES

Stop – 1: slap.

Stop – 2: bury.

Stop – 3: turn.

by a new skill drill. The crew will enjoy rising to the challenge and will feel a sense of achievement on mastering the skill. If the skill has been well thought out by the coach then ultimately they will be more technical and precise in their rowing. An exercise designed to challenge the best scullers might be to pause on the recovery, just after the blades have been tapped down and pushed away. They might try holding both scull handles in one hand while lifting up one leg and the opposite arm, for example, and continue sculling fluently and repeat a few strokes later. This challenges coordination, core stability, balance and confidence.

How and Why Do Skill Drills Improve Rowing Efficiency?

At first glance it is possible to see these exercises as purely that and not adding to the skill of the crew. Learning how to balance the boat, what the tipping points are and how to maintain balance with minimal effort are vitally important. Feeling in control and realizing how much time there is for the stroke helps with skill. Enabling the rower to be confident in their ability at all stages of the stroke cycle is critical for good technique. Undertaking these exercises in crew boats can improve timing, an understanding of working together and helps to give confidence in all conditions and at all boat speeds. Ensure that if an exercise is not going well it is practised little and often or that a simpler form is undertaken until success is achieved. This will ensure that frustration at an inability to learn the skill does not hamper progress. There is a historical tendency to concentrate on training mileage, whether in a coastal or river context. Developing rower physiology is critical for rowing fast, but skill in the boat will undoubtedly increase efficiency and boat speed.

test for a crew boat. The best crews are able to achieve this. Hence when paddling or racing no added energy is wasted in balancing the boat and there is far less risk of injuries caused by compensating for each other. The timing should be perfect and this will be

reflected in the blade work during racing.

Challenging the Crew

Even the best rowers can be challenged

CHAPTER 7

ROWING TECHNIQUE

Good technique is about producing maximum power for minimum effort. The techniques required are dynamic, however, and change continually so a series of pictures can only give a snapshot of what is required to move a boat efficiently. Maximizing the distance by which the boat moves with each stroke is the most efficient and effective way to gain and maintain boat speed.

The way the oar works is detailed in Chapter 8 but this chapter deals with how the rower uses their body most effectively to produce power. Klaus Mattes described effective technique as being a 'physiological and biomechanical solution' to ensure the rower maximizes their potential to maintain boat speed no matter what the conditions. Differences in size, strength and ability mean that different rowers achieve their maximum efficiency in slightly different ways.

'Linking Together the Kinetic Chain'

Most of the concepts that contribute to efficient technique can be summed up in one or more of the pictures. However, the concept of 'linking together the kinetic chain' applies to the whole stroke. The rowing stroke requires constant movement and application of power or controlled recovery to be effective. The whole of the body is engaged in rowing, and each part of the body is a part of the chain that must link together to transfer power. Hence posture and trunk stability are key to rowing efficiently. (Core strength and how to achieve this and the links to technique are discussed in Part V.)

Sculling and Sweep Technique

The catch   This is the point where the blade changes direction and enters the water. It is a very small part of the stroke and so the rower must prepare for this on the recovery. The body is rocked over, the arms are straight and the rower's whole system will be under slight tension created by the core stabilizing muscles in order to apply a force once the blade is locked into the water. The spoon should be buried as quickly as possible by raising the hands and the feet start to 'load' the blade.

The drive   This uses the legs to initiate the movement and then the body and finally the shoulders and arms join in. This is where the kinetic chain is potentially at its most vulnerable, as the back must remain in a set position in the first part of the drive so the power from the legs can be transferred to the handle.

The extraction or finish   This is where the blade is taken out of the water. It is the second most vulnerable point at which the kinetic chain can break down. The body needs to maintain the pressure on the feet for as long as possible, until the blades are out of the water. If the body slumps at this point then the weight will come off the feet, back onto the seat too early and off the blades, therefore slowing the boat.

The recovery   This is when the body and blades return to the catch position. The slide sequencing for hands, body and legs are really important both to prepare for the catch and maximize boat speed in the recovery. Moving in the right way can add to boat speed and prepare the rower to take the next catch.

For Sculling

The left hand should remain in front and slightly above the right hand, and this relationship should be kept during the drive phase and the recovery. The hands should move into and out from the body at the same speed. As the stroke rate increases all movements speed up to maintain the same stroke ratio.

PHASES OF THE STROKE

Rowing is a cyclical action that should have a continuous flow and rhythm without pause. The phases of the stroke are:

- **the catch** – when the blade goes into the water;
- **the drive phase** – when the blade is in the water, using forces to propel the boat forward;
- **the extraction** – sometimes also called 'the finish', when the blade comes out of the water; and
- **the recovery** – when the rower prepares to take the next stroke.

The sculling sequence

LEFT AND BELOW: Sculling: the catch sequence.

LEFT AND BELOW: Sculling: the drive sequence.

RIGHT AND BELOW: Sculling: the drive sequence.

RIGHT AND BELOW: Sculling: the extraction sequence.

Sculling: the recovery sequence.

Sculling: the left hand is in front of and slightly on top of the right during the recovery.

For Sweep

For sweeping the inside hand controls the squaring and feathering of the blade. The inside hand also provides pressure against the pin, which aids the stability of the boat. The outside hand controls the height of the blade during the recovery and drive and 'takes' the catch.

The sweep sequence

LEFT AND BELOW:
Sweeping: the catch sequence.

LEFT AND OPPOSITE:
Sweeping: the drive sequence.

CHAPTER 8

PRINCIPLES OF MOVING A BOAT

The principles of moving a boat will be completely integrated into the technical model. Often technique is described and shown in terms of body and blade movements but understanding how this moves the boat should help the rower to apply their efforts more effectively. The most efficient way to move a boat from A to B is at a constant speed. This is impossible in a rowing boat because force is only applied intermittently during the phase when the blade is in the water. In addition, the mass of the rower moving backwards and forwards has a significant effect on boat speed. Much of the achievement of good technique is linked to maximizing efficiency and minimizing fluctuations in boat velocity and acceleration.

Resistance on the Hull

There are three main types of resistance on the boat that together account for up to 87 per cent of the total drag on the boat. They are form drag, wave drag and skin friction resistance. Wave drag is caused by the turbulence in the water of the boat moving forward and a wave will be created at the bow as the water parts and in the stern as the water comes back together. Wave drag gets bigger with an increase in speed, but rowing smoothly is the best way to contribute to minimizing this drag. Form drag is due to the shape of the boat, hence a smaller cross-section gives less form drag so a long and narrow profile works best. Finally skin friction causes a boundary layer of water to be dragged along by the boat. This layer is smallest at the bows and largest at the stern of the boat.

The length of the boat has to be able to provide longitudinal stability and this is why the more the weight the longer the boats are with a bigger cross-section.

There is not much that can be done to reduce drag apart from ensuring the crew row as smoothly as possible and row in the right weight boat for their size. Modern boat-builders already factor this into their design by determining appropriate overall boat length and cross section.

Since the boat designer and builder have already taken the drag factors into account there is little for the coach and crew to consider in this respect. However, the size of the boat and the centre of gravity of the crew mean that the boat only has static stability when it is upside down. The crew must therefore learn to balance the boat and restrict transverse rotation or rolling. Moving together and using the oars as a tightrope walker uses their poles is critical to achieve this – hence the importance of the skill drills to straight line boat speed.

Aerodynamic Drag

Some 13 per cent of the drag on the boat happens above the water line. This drag is made up of 15 per cent from the boat and riggers, 35 from the crew and 50 per cent from the oars. In a headwind this can increase by up to four times and decrease to zero in a strong tailwind. Ways to minimize this drag are to ensure that hair is tied up, the crew wear hats and that the clothes fit well enough not to flap in the wind. Seating the tallest person in the bows of the boat will reduce aerodynamic drag but this might also affect the trim of the boat and slow it down more than the aerodynamic drag. Within the rules of rowing little else can be achieved to counter aerodynamic drag.

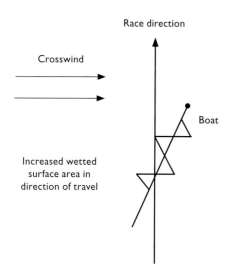

Race direction

Crosswind

Increased wetted surface area in direction of travel

Boat

Rowing in a strong crosswind.

Utilizing Energy Effectively

A rower's ability to produce power can be measured in the boat and also on an ergometer. It is not necessarily the rowers with the biggest work capacity who go the fastest. Rowing technique and how the power is applied are the most important aspects of moving the boat efficiently.

Moving the Boat

Power application to the blade moves the boat and it in turn acts as a lever. There are three orders of levers (Archimedes Laws) and two of these are used for moving a boat:

1. The first order lever is used during the catch and the recovery. At the catch a force is applied to the handle and there is a short period of time when the spoon is catching up with the speed of the water. During this period the pin is the fulcrum and the load is out on the spoon.
2. Once the spoon is moving at the same speed as the water the spoon becomes the fulcrum and the force is applied to the handle and the load is on the pin. Thus the blades work as second order levers.

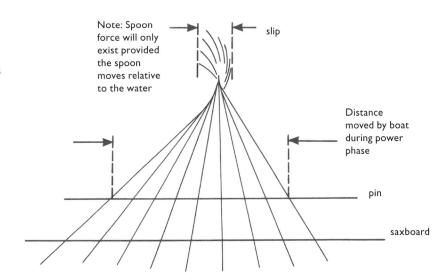

Note: Spoon force will only exist provided the spoon moves relative to the water

slip

Distance moved by boat during power phase

pin

saxboard

The blade path.

3. This first order lever is also used during the recovery when the handle is pushed away and moved through the air by the rower. The blade moves around the pin so the force is applied to the handle; the fulcrum is the swivel and the load is the spoon.

The pathway of the spoon

The pathway of the spoon in the

water during the drive phase of the stroke is important for how the two orders of lever are achieved. The mechanics of the blade are extremely complicated and are still not understood completely. Once the boat is moving the blades are catching moving water so the spoon tip moves forward and at the same time out from the centre line of the boat. Understanding the pathway the spoon describes and the angles is important so rowers are clear about how they can use this to move the boat most effectively.

At the catch for sculling the blade may be at an angle of 66–60 degrees in front of the 90-degree point to the boat. For sweep this will be in the region of 56–53 degrees. As already stated this means that the blade is moving out from the boat and if a simple lever system is applied this is very inefficient. Coaches will speak about pinching the boat and not getting too big an angle at the catch. (When effective international crews' catch angles are measured they are in the ranges given below.)

As the blade goes into the water the boat and blade system are moving

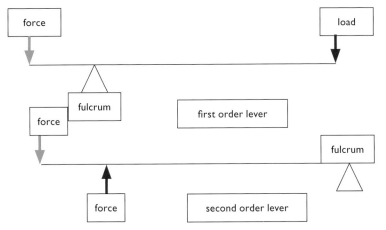

First order lever at the catch and recovery and second order lever during the drive once the spoon is loaded in the water.

Table 8   Optimal Angles (in Degrees) for Placement of the Blade for Different Classes of Boat

Boat class	Catch angle	Finish angle	Total angle
Men's Sculler	66	46	112
Men's Lwt Sculler	65	45	110
Men's Sweep	56	34	93
Men's Lwt Sweep	55	33	88
Women's Sculler	62	44	106
Women's Lwt Sculler	60	42	102
Women's Sweep	53	33	86

A quad scull showing how long the stroke is even after the blades are locked and buried.

forward in the water so effectively that the blade tip moves forward through the water rather than just out from the hull. This enables the blade to be used as a hydrofoil and to give lift in the first part of the stroke. Lift is very efficient but is only maintained in the early part of the stroke. The longer the stroke the longer this lift can be maintained and, although the blade must continue to move in order to achieve lift, this part of the stroke must not be hurried. Once the 'stalling position' for lift on the blade has been reached then it operates as a second order lever. At the finish of the stroke there is stored energy on the shaft that helps the blade to 'flick out' of the water. This description of how the blade works was first described by Jumbo Edwards as long ago as 1963 in his book *The Way of a Man with a Blade*.

The diagram in this section shows the pathway of the blade in the water. Also shown is the slip. This is the distance the blade moves in the water but reducing the slip to zero is not possible or desirable as slip is required to maintain load on the blade.

As the boat is moving through the water all rowers will lose some effective stroke length of between 5–20 degrees when getting their spoon in the water. There is a certain amount of air time required to get the blade to boat/water speed. As the stroke rate increases so the length of the stroke decreases, however good the crew. Once the blade is in the water it must be loaded as quickly as possible.

There are three reasons why top scullers and sweep rowers always appear to have time at the catch. First, the very large angles they row through mean that every 2cm of handle travel requires only 1cm of seat travel (see diagram). Second, this is where the best rowers take time to 'feel the load' and lock the blade. The rower should aim to sweep the blade at this point and not just get the handle into the body as quickly as possible, thus maximizing the 'lift' on the blade. Third, the boat is moving at its slowest just after the catch so the load is large. This high load at the catch requires the rower to have good core strength to maintain the lumber-to-pelvic ratio and not to lose power in the kinetic chain. The lumber-to-pelvic ratio is the ability of the lumber spine to maintain a neutral position in relation to the pelvis and, more importantly, to maintain this throughout the whole of the stroke cycle (see Chapter 11).

Exercises such as the front stop roll ups are essential for practising placing and loading the blade. Other front stops exercises can be used to work on placement and loading while the boat is moving. The same applies to long front-loaded strokes in sweep rowing boats. The large angles enable the rower to grip the water effectively but it is a highly technical part of the stroke so must be practised. The rower must understand how the blade works and what it feels like to lock and load the blade effectively.

The splash on blade entry

There is much discussion about the splash on entry of the blade. However skilled the rower it will not be possible to cover the blade in the water instantly, but the more skilled the rower the smaller the entry splash will be. A coach may speak about taking the catch while coming forward in order to ensure the rower is ready to cover the blade when the maximum forward position has been reached. The ideal blade entry is to catch the water in

Initial splash to the bows and then the second part of the entry to the stern

Entry splash.

time with the speed of the boat. This means some splash towards the bow on the initial catch and then towards the stern on the second part of the bury to show they have caught up with the water speed.

Boat Acceleration

Although the movement of the rower in the boat is cyclical and rhythmical the boat does not move at an even pace. A typical acceleration trace of the boat will show the boat at its slowest just after the catch and at its fastest on the start of the recovery (which is as soon as the body starts to move forward and is continued once the seat moves). This is partially as a result of timing, the need for the crew to change direction and the way the power is applied to the boat. Much of rowing technique is about minimizing energy losses during the rowing phases, thus trying to ensure there are not huge fluctuations in boat speed and changes of direction are smooth and well timed. As rowing takes place in a fluid, roughly nine times the power has to be applied to go twice as fast. Fluctuations in boat speed occur as the crew move their centre of gravity as their mass is far greater than that of the boat. Smooth, efficient movements at all times are critical and will lead to less effort being required for the same boat speed.

Acceleration trace

The boat acceleration trace and force profile from the rower (see below) are overlaid with the catch and extraction/finish points of the stroke marked (see diagram). When the boat speed is at its lowest the rower can exert maximum force and as the boat speed increases so the ability to keep the force high diminishes.

Force Profile

A rower's force profile is very individual and will vary slightly depending on the

boat being rowed. Force profiles can be generated from sensors on the blade or pin in one or two directions. The blade measurements are more accurate but often more complicated to set up. The key factor to consider is the area under the curve, which is the impulse. The impulse is determined by an integration of force and force with time. Increasing the magnitude of the force while maintaining the time or vice versa will lead to a greater impulse and potentially a faster-moving boat. Therefore a long duration and forceful stroke will produce maximum boat speed. A good force profile is one where the peak force is reached before the 90-degree (or orthogonal) angle to the boat. For reasons already discussed the force will take time to build, but reaching 70 per cent of maximum force by 30 per cent of the stroke's length will give good acceleration to the boat. A smooth force profile is best – so no sudden, jerky moves – and maintaining force in the second half of the stroke will also contribute to overall boat speed.

The time graph here shows how quickly the rower is able to apply the force. This is a combination of getting the blade buried and locked into the water as quickly as possible. The reason the force goes up quickly is that the boat is moving at its slowest after the catch. As the boat speed increases the application of force cannot keep increasing. The important information to

> **COACHING POINT**
>
> It is important to note that the rower has to keep thinking about accelerating the handle through to the finish even though the peak acceleration is reached in the middle of the stroke. The application of force to the foot plate throughout the stroke is essential to keep the load on the blade. The force profile cannot be looked at in isolation but must be seen with the boat speed and acceleration.

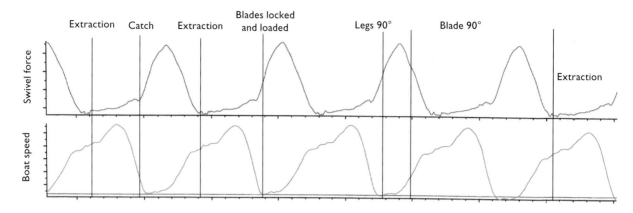

Swivel time/boat speed.

take from the typical profile is the overall shape: the force increases with a rate that ensures peak force is reached before the blade gets to the 90-degree angle. The length of the stroke and the peak force determine the total amount of power so a long duration and forceful, front-loaded, leg-driven stroke enables this to happen.

Energy Loss from Pitch, Roll and Yaw

Energy can be lost by the boat pitching, rolling or yawing. To observe the pitch, watch the bow ball (safety cap at the bow) and how it moves during the rowing stroke. The bow ball rises up from the water and then sinks back down again. This is the pitch on the boat. This is caused primarily by the movement of the crew and the power application on the blade. The pitch can be linked to boat acceleration, and the timing of the catch can contribute to smoothing out the highs and the lows of the acceleration.

Rolling is when the boat dips alternately to starboard or port. It can often produce disagreements in a crew and particularly in a sweep boat can be very uncomfortable and disruptive to timing and, ultimately, steering. All boats roll but the best rowers can minimize

this and have enough skill to time the catch together in sweep or sculling boats.

Yaw is when the stern of the boat slides sideways. In a crosswind a boat may appear to be 'crabbing' its way forward. If rowing in lanes, look at the boat from ahead or astern: in extreme crosswind conditions the boat will appear to be at an angle of 15–20 degrees to the expected forward direction. Mistiming can lead to excessive yaw, with the consequent need to steer continually. Any yaw will mean that boat has covered extra distance due to steering and experiences an increase in drag due to the added wetted surface area in contact with the water in the direction of travel. All of this causes disruption to the straight line speed. Steering causes the boat to roll so yaw is often accompanied by roll.

Developing Technique

Good technique and how to achieve this have been described, as have confidence and technical exercises, in Chapters 6 and 7. However, random error is a natural part of learning a new skill; any skill development will go through a series of phases before being fully ingrained. The coach will need to determine which

errors are due to a lack of consistency and which are a result of poor application of technique. This is where the skill drills and technical challenges for the crew are important and can help to correct technique.

For all skill development a similar cycle of learning will be repeated, so in the first instance getting the boat on the water and effectively set up will for most rowers move them through all the stages of the model. For example, at first the rower will need help and probably instruction or questioning to get the boat and them onto the water. After a few more tries the learner will make mistakes but should be able to identify these and how to correct them. After a few more tries the learner is usually competent but still has to concentrate on what they are doing. Finally, they can get the boat out on the water and automatically react to slight variations in the situation without thinking about it.

This process is the equivalent of getting one's car out of the garage and onto the road so is a fairly simple skill. As a learner progresses the skills they acquire will become more complicated with other elements such as the environment, other crew members and other water users all impacting on the delivery. As more skills are developed so the rower will again move through each of these phases of the conscious competence model. Only the most skilful and the ones who consciously develop their skills will be able to row a high speed race in rough crosswind conditions and remain technically competent.

Technical Drills to Aid Sequencing

The stroke sequence has been described previously (see Chapter 7) but there are other exercises in the boat that can be used to develop sequencing.

Roll ups   The crew or sculler sit at backstops with their blades buried. They use the normal hands–body slide sequence and speed to come to the catch position and bury the blade. This develops: the recovery sequence; balance skills (since the boat is at its most unstable when stationary); confidence to place the blade at the catch; confidence to load the blade; and assurance that the rower can reach the catch position without rushing into frontstops. A development once the recovery and placement are efficient is to take a stroke. The boat should be stationary before the next roll up is executed. A good variation on roll ups to practice the recovery sequence at race rate.

Suspension   The rower must be able to apply their weight onto the handle and maintain this through the whole drive phase. Providing the sequencing of the drive is correct and the kinetic chain is maintained, then the more weight suspended on the handle the faster the boat will go. The most basic suspension exercise is for the rower to sit in the catch position with the blades buried. If they back down the boat for a few inches and then change direction to take a stroke they will be able to feel the load. This exercise can also include lifting off the seat. Providing the blade is locked into the water throughout the whole stroke the rower will be able to maintain the suspension to the end of the stroke

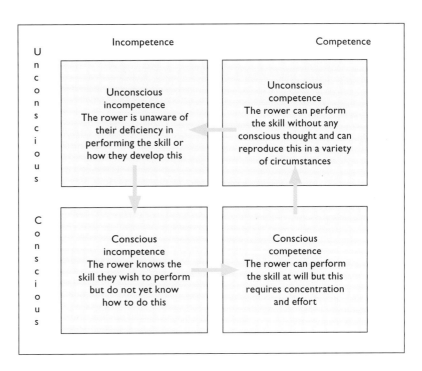

The conscious competence model.

and return lightly to the decking. Ensure the rowers are not lifting with the body but are using their gluteal muscles and legs and pushing through the feet. Once the rower can achieve this while backing down then progress to doing it with a stationary boat. Try to get the suspension as early in the drive phase as possible. Engage the gluteal muscles to get the lift rather than just using the quadriceps.

Suspension using the ergometer   Fixed-head ergometers can be used very effectively to teach suspension. Tie the handle in the catch position firmly to the cage and get the rower to sit at the catch and lift their weight off the seat. This should be achieved by squeezing the gluteal muscles and going straight up. If the rower extends their legs to achieve suspension then they are using the quadriceps muscles. Using the gluteal muscles early in the drive will create a

more powerful and more sustainable drive. (Note that this is more complicated to demonstrate on a moving-head ergometer.)

Sequencing   Rowing technique requires correct sequencing of the legs, body, and arms in the drive. This exercise is designed to assist the rower by progressively adding in legs, body and arms to the movement. The rower should sit in the catch with the blades buried and initially just raise the lower the blade. This should go from buried to just above the water, and repeat. Make sure the blades on both sides of the boat are sychronized. This movement should come from the arms raising and lowering from the shoulder and not from the wrists or elbows. The next stage is to take the first 6in of the stroke by covering the blade and then just pushing with the feet and slightly extending the knees. Ensure the rower has not moved their body or bent theit arms. Then this should be repeated for the quarter-slide, half-slide, three-quarter-slide and full slide. For all of this the body and arms are not used other than to transfer power so the body is still at the catch angle and the arms are still straight. There will be a point in this sequence where the rower feels the legs suddenly go down with little resistance and this is the where the body should come in.

The next phase is to bring in the body but still with the arms straight. The final sequence is when the arms join in and complete the full stroke. As this exercise takes quite a long time then between five and ten strokes in each phase is appropriate. If in a crew boat then the other crew members should be sitting the boat, or in a sweep boat the exercise is completed in pairs. The boat will be heavy and it will be easier for the rower to get the sequence and load the blade from early in the drive. As they will not be able to push out quickly this is a good time to experiment with locking and loading as two separate actions although with no pause between them. If the other crew members join in the sequence gradually then the rower will be challenged to maintain the sequence in the faster-moving boat. Repeat this until all members of the crew have completed the exercise.

Pause rowing   This can assist the crew with timing as they have to arrive at a certain point in the stroke at the same time. For a sculler this can still give them time to ensure the sequencing has been correct and will give them confidence. The most usual and easiest place for a pause is in the 'easy all' or 'safe' position. This can be changed to the finish once the blades are out of the water or any position on the recovery slide including the catch position. A double pause can also be included (so 'finish' and 'hands away', for example, if this part of the sequence is not very coordinated). Do not hold the pause too long or the blades will hit the water and disrupt any chance of coordinated and sequenced rowing.

Crew timing   This is crucial, or the crew will always feel rushed or unbalanced. The best crews will practise timing and can perform very intricate exercises in a stationary boat. This can include multiple roll ups to different points in the stroke with perfect synchronicity and balance. Alternatively exercises on the run, which can include holding the scull handles in one hand and lifting legs or arms or putting the sweep blade beneath the foot and waving the arms, are also possibilities. The important things are to challenge the crew and to have fun.

The correct grip   How to hold the blade was described in Chapter 3 but for the novice rower this must be continually re-enforced or they will struggle with technique, especially hanging their weight on the blade. Exercises exist in sculling to help roll the blade into the fingers, relax the grip on the handle, keep the wrists flat and ensure that the left hand is slightly on top and leading during the recovery. Try opening the fingers on the recovery, as this helps to ensure that the grip is correct and the wrist is flat. To ensure the left hand leads away just open the fingers of the left hand on the recovery (just this action usually ensures the left hand leads out from the finish).

The role of the inside/outside hand   The roles of the different hands can be practised in sweep rowing. An example of this might be rowing with the inside hand on the recovery and the outside hand during the drive. The outside hand controls the blade height and the inside hand the squaring and feathering. If the crew are not 'catching' with the outside hand or feathering the blade on the recovery with the inside hand then ask them to undertake this activity. As they approach the catch with the blade square, the inside hand comes off the blade for the drive. The outside hand taps down, and after the recovery has started the inside hand comes onto the handle to feather and square the

blade and then repeat. This exercise enables the crew to consider the role of each hand and can be fun to learn to do as a group.

Square blade rowing   This requires the crew to be more precise in their finish, recovery and catch positions. Timing the entry and exit and moving together is the only way the boat will be balanced. Variations on this can include one stroke feathered, one square; or portside feathered and starboard side square and vice versa. This can be a very frustrating exercise if the crew keep catching the blades on the recovery due to timing or oar recovery heights. In this case initiate the exercise with only one square blade stroke and gradually build this up. Frustration tends to lead to tension, which causes rowers to move less fluidly and in turn this exacerbates the problem.

Eyes closed rowing   This requires the crew to feel and listen to the movement in the boat. It can help the rower to start to feel how to row, which is important in the conscious competence cycle of learning a skill.

Rhythm and ratio   These are important and at low rating the crew will be taking longer on the recovery than during the drive phase. Some rowers have a tendency to rush and so exercises such as 'eyes closed' can help them to feel the boat running under them. Thinking about the feet coming to them rather than rushing over the feet can help to slow down the recovery. Counting a rhythm and trying to count from one to three or four on the recovery and one to two on the drive can help. Singing can also relax the crew and make them more rhythmical throughout the whole stroke.

Using sounds   If there is a part of the stroke where the timing is particularly poor getting the whole crew to say 'now' at that point can really help (typically this will be the finish or the catch). Ask the crew to all say 'now' as they come out of the water. Initially this may be as many 'nows' as rowers in the boat. Gradually the crew will get closer together and the timing will improve. This can be used for any part of the stroke – starting to move up the slide on the recovery or placing the blade at the catch are other examples.

Slaps on the catch   These can help the rower to lift their hands and also to take their time at the catch. The rower or crew arrive in the catch position and with the blade still feathered they slap the blade on the water and then quickly square it and take the catch. This can also help a rower who may be slow or not very definite about locking the blade in the water at the catch.

Improving relaxation   The relaxation necessary to catch the water and have a lose grip can be achieved by rowing full strokes and about every ten strokes asking the rower to take three quick strokes but from backstops and arms only. In order to catch the water the rower must be really relaxed and move quickly to bury the blade.

All these exercises and many more must be explained accurately to the rower and they must know why they are undertaking the exercise. Drills are not there just for the sake of it but each one can be used in a multitude of ways to help develop timing, balance, skill, and much more. A rower with the right focus is much more likely to improve than one who has no idea of the desired outcome from the drill.

PART IV

PSYCHOLOGY AND NUTRITION

CHAPTER 9

PSYCHOLOGY

This chapter focuses on managing the mind during training and racing. In the past there was a tendency to see psychology as an 'add on' rather than being just as important as technique or fitness training. Psychology should be delivered as part of the longitudinal training programme.

Often delivered via the coach, there are ways of working that can impact on the ability of the rower to learn, train and (if racing) to perform under pressure. Physical and mental capacity are intrinsically linked so getting the mindset right is fundamental.

Know Yourself

Rowers and coaches are individuals who will each have a different approach to learning and communication. If as a rower or coach you understand your preferences and those of the group then you can ensure the best learning

Psychology is important for training and racing.

environment is created for the benefit of everyone. Knowing what motivates you and how you build your confidence can improve your ability stick to the training and build your self-esteem or increase your performance achievements.

When you are learning a new skill do you like to see what you are doing, hear what it sounds like or feel how the body executes the movement? Most of us are visual learners and so like to see and watch what we are doing. For this group of learners, seeing images and video of the correct technique and their efforts in comparison to this, will have very good results for improving skill development and technique. By contrast aural learners (those who like to hear what they are doing) will respond to hearing the noise of the rowing stroke and the boat movement. Demonstrating the correct methods including the element of sound is important when introducing a new skill. Finally, the kinesthetic rowers like to feel what they are doing. Feeling all aspects of the rowing stroke and storing the right movement sequencing is vital to ensure the correct technique is applied to all aspects of the stroke. Often a rower or coach will reveal their preference by the words they use, so a visual learner will refer to seeing, an aural learner to hearing and a kinesthetic learner to feeling.

Eventually all good rowers will 'feel' how the boat moves and make automatic corrections. Chapter 8 discussed the conscious competence learning model with the cyclical learning that takes place for acquiring each new skill. The most skillful rowers can feel what happens and unconsciously make the right adjustments for the current conditions. Understanding what type of learner you are will help to ensure you take advantage of the best cues for you. Realizing that ultimately you need to 'feel' what is happening enables you to start to think about how the movements feel. Using a variety of coaching methods and words related to the various learning styles will have the best impact on the whole group.

Using technology to give rowers feedback.

Deliberately linking in 'feeling' with the visual or aural sounds will help learners to be conscious of their need to engage this sense.

Motivation

Rowing is a demanding sport physically, mentally and emotionally. As many rowers fit training around other aspects of life this can mean early starts, late finishes and long weekends spent down at the river. It is important, therefore, to understand why each person has turned to rowing. If you can understand the motivations of the individual you can tailor the coaching and programme to help keep the rower motivated. As a rower it is equally important to understand what motivates you to keep attending the early mornings and weekend training sessions.

Motivation can change over time as personal circumstances change. Just getting fitter, enjoying time on the river or spending time with friends may be the initial motivation to start rowing. For some this will never change, whereas others may discover their competitive streak or decide to train more frequently or harder. The reverse can also happen as an individual's life circumstances change and they move from a competitive rower to one who uses rowing for recreation and keeping fit. Personal challenges such as completing a day's tour or a distance on the water may be the end goal. Setting different types of goals with short-, medium- and long-term timescales as appropriate can help with motivation.

Know how you respond to motivation. Are you most likely to achieve a goal if working as part of a crew and working hard for the team? Or are you at your best when you are in charge and watching the numbers on the dial of an ergometer and responding appropriately? Are you motivated from an external source such as encouragement from or technical calls from a coxswain or coach? Whichever of these describes you ensure that you factor this way of motivating yourself into your training programme. All important for keeping your motivation and focus is goal setting.

Goal Setting

There are three types of goals, which relate to outcome, performance and process. By setting all three types there is more chance that all will be achieved. Goals should also be set for the short-, medium- and long-term and they also should be set using the SMART principles. As in every aspect of life, if you have an aim to meet, whether relating to performance or leisure, then motivation is likely to remain high for a sustained period of time.

Understanding the motivation of the coach is as important as understanding that of the rower. Whether professional or volunteer, coaches should involve rowers in the goal-setting process. If the goals are those of the coach and not the rowers then they are unlikely to be achieved. Goals and motivation should be in line for the rower and their coach in order for their relationship to work. In order to achieve a positive outcome it is important that goal setting for coach and rowers is undertaken to determine the aims of individuals and make sure they all align.

Outcome Goals

The outcome goal is related to an aspiration and, while this may be inspirational, it is not within the control of the rower. Such goals may relate to winning a race or a medal, or, at one extreme, might be to complete a

record crossing of the Atlantic. For those new to the sport it may be winning their first race or completing advanced skills in a crew boat. Winning a race will also be dependent on the quality of the opposition, however, so the rower may have executed their best race possible but have been beaten by a better rower on the day. Weather will play a big factor in setting records for crossing the Atlantic, for example, even if all other aspects of the planning and crew fitness have been meticulous.

Performance Goals

The performance goal is related to a specific outcome and is measurable against a previous performance. Completing a 2,000m ergometer performance in a better time than before, or sitting with the blades off the water for a longer time in the skills tests, would be examples of performance goals. Achieving performance goals enables the rower to come closer to achieving their outcome goal.

The performance goal can help the rower to stay focused and lead them continually to improve their level in each session. How fast an ergometer test is completed will give evidence of potential boat speed. How fast a 2,000m race is completed and how boat speed is monitored in training is determined by the time measured. This will provide the evidence to the rower that they have the ability to row at the standard they have aspired to reach.

Process Goals

The process goal is possibly the most important goal type but is often overlooked. Process goals usually relate to technical and skill development, tactics, mental development or even rower welfare issues such as getting enough rest and

recovery. Achieving the process goals should lead to the ability to achieve the performance goals. The process goal gives focus for an area of improvement and keeps the rower's attention in the here and now.

All Goals Should Be SMART

Specific   The goal must be specific in nature, whether it is an outcome, performance or process goal. Examples of specific goals might include making a certain time on the water or ergo, or achieving a position in a race or certain performance level such as participating at Henley, becoming a National Champion or rowing internationally.

Measurable   How do you know when you have achieved your goal? How will it be measured? In order to know you are on track there should be some milestones and interim testing on the way.

Achievable   Any goal should be challenging but achievable. Do not put success out of reach and ensure that you set short-, medium- and long-term goals. The 'A' here can also stand for adjustable since you need to be flexible and review your goals and, if necessary, adjust. So achieving a goal ahead of time or at a higher level, for example, may require a further goal to be set.

Realistic   Be realistic that the goal you set yourself is right for you. Variables to consider include how much time you can devote to training, the quality of your training and the level at which you currently perform.

Time Based   The goal should be based on a period of time. If there is no timescale in which to achieve it there will be less attention given to it and the urgency to make it happen will be lost.

GOAL SETTING FOR DIFFERENT TYPES OF ROWER

Example 1: Goal Setting for an International Rower

At international level an outcome goal may be winning an Olympic medal, in which case performance goals such as ergometer achievements will feature heavily. A further performance goal may be the time for a 2,000m time trial in ideal conditions. Just as important are the process goals, which may include perfecting the sequencing on the stroke recovery, correctly executing the first two strokes of a race and others examples similar to this. The performance goal for the 2,000m time trial is more likely to be achieved if each process in the race is practised and in the control of the rower. The same applies to the outcome goal; if all the performance goals are achieved then the outcome is more likely to be achieved.

Example 2: Goal Setting for a Club Competitive Rower

An outcome goal may be to win the Wyfolds at Henley Royal Regatta or the club fours at Henley Women's Regatta. A performance goal related to this might be a specific boat speed for the distance of the race. Process goals might relate to the quality of aerobic training on the water, sequencing the stroke correctly, burying the blade more quickly on the catch and keeping focused in your own boat. Training time will need to be in line with the aspiration, as a well-devised and well-executed programme can deliver a performance. The process and performance goals can really help to keep the rower motivated if they can see how they relate to their chance of achieving their ultimate outcome goal.

Example 3: Goal Setting for a Recreational Rower

Recreational rowers will be motivated to learn to row as a new skill. An outcome goal may be to take out the boat and complete a training session independently. Performance goals related to this might be to complete all the skill tests to a certain level as agreed with the coach. Process goals might include being able to get the boat onto the water and adjust appropriately, being able to steer the boat and navigate obstacles, row with blades off the water and able to turn the boat in tight spaces. These skill sets will all enable the rower to gain more independence as an athlete and could be the motivating factor when taking up the sport. It is important that the skill levels increase in difficulty so the rower becomes more confident about what they are doing and how they are able to do it. If a rower feels they have nothing left to learn or achieve they will quickly lose the motivation that made them start the sport in the first place.

The skills outlined in Chapter 6 can be used to test the progress of those new into the sport. They have a specific aim to improve skill and technique, they are measurable, achievable, realistic and the timescale is determined by the timing of the exercise but also a knowledge of how quickly rowers can develop these skills. These tests can vary from how many rigger dips can be performed in a minute, for example, to how quickly a single can be spun a full 360-degree turn. Improvements on these types of skill require boat confidence but also specific practice.

Reviewing Performance

The problem with the outcome goal is that the rower has relatively little control over it. If the goal is winning a medal, for example, and they happen to be in an event with three other outstanding crews, they may not achieve this goal. Hence why it is so important to measure performance and analyze what happened in an event in various ways. Was the process right? Was the mindset right? If so then the perhaps the outcome goals, performance goals, and process goals were not sufficiently aligned, or as a rower you met an opponent who was better than you on the day. Rowers should develop the skills to analyze a training session or performance without looking at the numbers or the outcome.

When training or performing on an ergometer the split time is always shown. If the split falls below the one the rower expected then this can have a very negative effect on the overall performance. There may be other external reasons for the performance, such as previous training sessions, hydration status and preparation. The rower should do a training session without the dial being visible and respond to how their body feels for the training intensity. Equally, in a head race before the result is known the rowers will often make a good analysis of the performance. Once the results are published this will influence their analysis. In side-by-side racing it is important to focus on the process and what is happening in your boat. Constantly watching the opposition will not influence their rowing but will detract from your own. In the first part of the race focus totally on your

CHAPTER 10

NUTRITION

This chapter focuses on ensuring the body is fuelled and ready to go for training and racing. This requires a basic understanding of what foods contain in order to understand what to eat and drink and when.

Eating a varied and healthy diet together with maintaining hydration is important for optimizing training and racing opportunities. Many rowers and coaches consider that exercise programmes require a specialist diet, which might include supplements. If basic nutrition is correct then most rowers will only need to consider when and what they are going to eat and drink throughout the day to optimize their pre-training status and post-training recovery. To have a balanced diet, food must be taken from each of the food groups in appropriate proportions. Understanding what foods and hence which nutrients are in each of the groups will lead to informed choices. There is a plethora of information available about creating a balanced diet but do ensure the information you draw on comes from a reputable and reliable source.

Supplements and Anti-doping

The British Rowing anti-doping policy, which can be found on their website, states 'British Rowing condemns the use of doping in sport'. This statement goes on to speak about the role of education and testing in ensuring that rowing and rowers remain drug free. Anti-doping follows a strict liability rule meaning that the rower is responsible for anything found in their system.

In order to remain drug free the rower should understand a few basic facts about drug-free sport. In over 50 per cent of cases involving the Anti-doping Agency the athletes were unaware that the substance they had taken contained a banned substance. Many sportsmen and women take a morning vitamin pill or the occasional herbal remedy. Are you aware that this could be making you a drug cheat? This may sound a bit dramatic but supplements are not regulated in the same way as medical drugs. This includes supplements sourced from well-known high street companies and over-the-counter medicines. If the innocent tablet has been made on a production line that previously had a product with a banned substance or the manufacturer has used other ingredients to flavour or bind the product together then any of these could lead to traces of a banned substance being detected.

Only supplements that are batch tested should be taken by the rower, and all others should be avoided. This includes all sports drinks, caffeine sports drinks, vitamin products and protein powders – unless they have been batch tested. Batch testing is undertaken by a reputable laboratory that is regulated by the UK Anti-doping Agency. Beware of items bought online appearing to be batch tested when this may not be the case. Most rowers do not require any supplements, which is why it is more important to focus here on advice relating to a balanced and appropriate diet. Many products such as caffeine drinks are not going to make a difference to performance and they can lead to all sorts of unwanted side effects. For those under 18 years old any supplements apart from a sports drink for longer training sessions should be discouraged.

The Body's Requirements for Rowing

The amount of food required by a rower to train successfully will depend on the rowers' age, gender, body weight and other daily activities. Add into this mix specific information such as any goals to reduce body mass or increase muscle bulk and the amount of training sessions undertaken per week and this will vary considerably between individuals. The number of calories burnt by international rowers ranges from 3500–6000 calories a day depending on gender, status as lightweight or open weight, plus current training intensity. Most part-time rowers will burn far fewer calories than this. Continuous and moderate rowing on a machine for an hour, for example, may burn 450–1000 calories on top of the recommended daily allowance for an active person of 2000 calories for women and 2500 for men. The rower will need to work out their nutritional requirements to maintain quality training.

It is best to consult with an expert as advice on nutrition will be very individual depending on circumstances, training loads and other daily activities. A dietician will also be able to give advice about ideal body weight ranges.

Monitoring Using a Food Diary

Much has been written about the balance of the essential food groups and the ideal proportions from each group. There is advice on the number of calories required per day but this is based on Mr and Mrs Average in terms of size, age and activity levels. A person undertaking training will require more calories if they wish to maintain their weight and obviously less if they wish to reduce it. A far better way of working out what is appropriate for the individual is to set a goal of weight management and work out the amount of exercise and how many additional calories this will require. By keeping a food diary and monitoring morning weight over a three to four week period adjustments to the diet can be made to achieve the desired goal and to fuel performance effectively.

Body Mass Index can be established for an individual and can be calculated easily using bodyweight and height. Remember that for young people body mass is expected to rise as the youngster grows. Rowers should be aiming to be within the healthy range for their height and weight. Calculating daily food requirements will need to be assessed over a period of weeks. If with training bodyweight climbs or drops then adjust the food intake accordingly. If bodyweight is dropping then review refuelling strategies and the timing of snacks and meals throughout the day. If bodyweight is increasing then the review how many calories are being consumed. There are often hidden calories in juices and sports drinks that will all need to be considered in the daily food intake.

Most rowing training sessions are in the range of 45 minutes to 90 minutes and the main fuel used by the body for the likely intensity and length of training sessions is glycogen, which is stored in the muscles and liver. There is a limited store of glycogen in the body so ensuring that levels are at optimum before and after training is important. Nutrition in terms of what will be eaten and when needs to be planned for training and racing. Race days often mean there is limited time between rounds and as each round gets harder the rower wants to be in the best possible state of readiness to produce a good performance.

Nutrients

Food provides a variety of nutrients that are essential to sustain life and grow and repair the body. There are three macronutrients that must be consumed in fairly large quantities since they provide the major tools for energy and regeneration. The three macronutrients are carbohydrates (which provide the body with energy), protein (needed for growth and repair) and fats (which contain essential fatty acids and fat-soluble vitamins). Eating a variety of food types from each macronutrient group will ensure the necessary range of vitamins and minerals, also known as micronutrients, are incorporated into the diet. In addition the body requires water and fibre to function effectively and remain healthy.

Carbohydrates

Carbohydrates (also referred to as CHO owing to their composition from carbon, hydrogen and oxygen molecules) are the main source of energy and are contained in starchy foods such as pasta, breads, rice, potatoes, breakfast cereal, cous cous and other grains, pulses including beans and lentils, root vegetables and fruit, and, finally, milk products. While CHO play a vital role in day-to-day living, for a rower they are essential to fuel training. Prolonged continuous activity of over 45 minutes will typically deplete the glycogen stores and most rowing sessions are longer than this.

CHO enters the bloodstream at different rates depending on its composition and also other foods ingested at the same time. CHO foods that are high in fibre and water will be absorbed more slowly by the body and the total CHO will be lower. Foods in this category are described as having a low glycaemic index (GI) and include fruit, vegetables, pulses, whole wheat grains and nuts. This group of foods is good for sustaining the glycogen levels in the muscles and liver as their CHO is released slowly over time. High to medium glycaemic index foods include bread, rice, potatoes, juices and sports drinks. A CHO that is released into the bloodsteam relatively quickly will cause a high level of insulin release, which means the CHO goes directly into the muscles. During exercise although insulin is not released the muscles are still able to take up the CHO. Therefore high to medium GI CHOs are good to use during or following exercise while low GI foods are good at all other times. Rowers need to eat a range of CHO in order to maximize their readiness to train and recover and also to get a range of micronutrients.

The body is unable to hold any more than around 350g of glycogen at one point and once it has reached full capacity any excess glucose will be converted into fat. If there is inadequate fuel in the body then the rower will feel fatigued, with the feeling that training is a big effort. If this occurs in the competitive period then the racing performance will be below potential. A lack of carbohydrate can also lead to impairment of the immune system.

There is a need to fuel up in the preceding one or two hours before training. If multiple sessions are being undertaken in the day then it becomes very important to refuel to ensure proper recovery before the next session.

When planning the type and timing of refuelling considerations to take into account are the type and intensity of training, the frequency of training sessions and the time available to recover. Body composition goals, such as the desire to build muscle or lose fat, are considerations. Environmental conditions such as cold weather can also affect the amount of CHO required. Other relevant considerations are family background and the performance goals for the season. This means that the amount of CHO and other nutrients in

Table 9   Carbohydrate Requirements for Different Training Intensities

Training Intensity	CHO required per kg of Body Mass
Light: low intensity or skill based	3–5g
Moderate: moderate intensity	5–7g
High: endurance programme of 1–3 hours per day	6–10g
Very high: extreme training involving multiple sessions totalling 4–5 hours per day	8–12g

the diet must be in line with the training volume.

If the training session is 45 minutes or less then there is no need to take CHO during training. If a session is over 45 minutes or part of multiple sessions for the day then some CHO during training

Table 10   Examples of 50g CHO Portions

Cereals

200g pasta

100g bread (3–4 slices)

180g boiled rice

60g cereals

Vegetables

350g potatoes

440g baked beans

Fruit

350g grapes

2 medium to large bananas

70g raisins/sultanas

500g fruit salad

Dairy

1ltr milk

560ml flavoured milk

Fruit juice and sports products

600ml unsweetened

500ml sweetened

700ml sports drink

1–1.5 sports bars

250ml CHO loader

may be required. This can be in the form of sports drinks or gels. There is a window in the first 15–20 minutes after training when the CHO is best taken up and stored by the body in the muscle cells. A good amount to aim for is 50g until a proper meal can be taken.

Protein

Protein is essential for structural and functional roles in the body. Connective tissue, cell membranes and muscle cells are all derived and repaired by protein. Enzymes and transport vehicles such as red blood cells and hormones are proteins. Endurance athletes in heavy training require more protein and for athletes wishing to gain muscle strength there may be a need for additional protein. During periods of heavy strength work more protein may be required. Protein consists of twenty-two amino acids, of which ten are essential (they must be taken in food as the body is unable to produce them).

Recreational rowers need the same level of protein as the general public, so 0.8–1.0g per kilogramme of body mass per day. A rower undertaking between four and six sessions of over 60 minutes per week may need to increase their intake to 1.2g/kg per day. Women require 15 per cent less protein per kilogramme per day than men.

Like CHO, protein is best replaced immediately after training. Consuming

CHO and protein together is the ideal combination. This could be in the form of a flavoured yoghurt, milk drinks, fruit smoothies or breakfast cereal with milk. Most people already have enough protein in their diet but those on a restrictive diet or those who do not consume a good range of foods may be in danger of not having enough. Consider when in the day you take protein in your diet as if training is early in the day taking in at least some protein at this point would be beneficial.

Iron

When planning the diet it is important to consider the iron content of food. A training rower needs higher levels of iron than an average person as the increase in blood volume and red blood cells require more iron. Iron is also lost in sweat. Activities with a high impact like running can reduce the numbers of red blood cells by damaging them. Anyone over reliant on snacks or not eating 'fortified with vitamins' cereals will also be at risk from low iron levels.

Iron from food comes in two forms: heam iron or non-heam iron. Heam iron is more easily taken in by the body and is contained in animal foods such as meat, fish and chicken. Non-heam iron is in non-animal foods such as breakfast cereal, wholemeal bread, spinach, dried apricots and nuts. In order to maximize the uptake of non-heam iron these foods should ideally be accompanied by Vitamin C, such as that contained in an orange juice drink.

Fat

Fat is an essential component of any diet as it helps the body to absorb nutrients as well as being a great source of energy. Essential fatty acids are contained in fat and the body is unable to manufacture these

Table 11   Foods Containing 10g Protein

Animal Products	Non-Animal Products
2 small eggs	4 slices wholemeal bread
300ml cow's milk	330g cooked pasta
200g yoghurt	400g cooked rice
30g cheese	60g nuts and seeds
40g chicken	400ml soya milk
50g grilled fish	150g legumes or lentils

independently. However, though fats are important we should attempt to monitor how much of them we are eating, as large amounts could lead to excess weight gain and could subsequently result in an increased risk of serious health concerns such as heart disease and high blood pressure. All fat contains both saturated and unsaturated fatty acids, though they are usually referred to as either 'saturated' or 'unsaturated' depending on the percentage of fatty acids present. Saturated fats are commonly found in animal products and processed foods such as meat, dairy and chips, and the unsaturated are found in foods such as avocados, olives, nuts and oily fish. It is good to aim to eat fish twice a week including oily fish at least once.

The structure of saturated and unsaturated fat is very different. Saturated fat is not considered to be healthy for the heart and is known to raise your LDL (bad) cholesterol levels. Unsaturated fats on the other hand are considered to be heart healthy and can actually work to lower your LDL cholesterol levels as well as raising your HDL (good) cholesterol levels.

Hydration

Just as important as food intake is the need to keep hydrated. Sweating is an important aspect of regulating the body's core temperature. 'Normal' body temperature is 37°C and

evaporation of sweat cools the body when necessary to maintain this.

Dehydration is defined as occurring when there is a 1 per cent or greater loss of bodyweight due to loss of fluid. Any amount of fluid loss will impair performance, however, as the table here shows. The 2 per cent loss defined as 'impaired performance' includes a breakdown in the ability to perform skills and to concentrate. These will be the noticeable signs to the coach but physiologically there will also be a decrease in cardiovascular function and the ability to regulate temperature. If the rower is to get the best out of the training sessions then avoiding this dehydrated state is imperative. Dehydration will alter the feel of how hard the session is and will lead ultimately to a switch in fuel use from glycogen to protein resulting in the break down of muscle.

The rower should drink in every session and the exact make-up of the

fluid should be dependent on the level of training required and performance goals. Drinking for performance is important for two aspects: first, to replace the fluid and sodium lost in the sweat; second, to ensure the body has enough glycogen to fuel the muscles for longer or for parts of a multiple training session. Any training session up to 45–60 minutes in length does not require any CHO in the drink, unless this is one of multiple sessions in the day. Longer or more intense training sessions will require additions to the water to maximize the body's ability to hydrate and to provide the glycogen required for training. CHO in the drink may enhance the body's ability to rehydrate.

Sodium chloride (salt) is also lost with sweat so this must be replaced either in the drink or with food and snacks after the session. A small pinch of salt is enough and snacks may well contain enough salt without the need to add more. Most breads already contain salt, for example. The presence of salt when rehydrating encourages the body to keep on taking in liquid whereas just drinking water may lead to the body refusing more liquid before being properly hydrated.

Determining Sweat Loss

A weigh-in before and after each training session can determine how much sweat is being lost in a typical session. This should be reviewed on a

Table 12   The Physiological Effects of Dehydration

% bodyweight lost as sweat	Physiological effect
2	Impaired performance.
4	Capacity for muscular work declines.
5	Heat exhaustion.
7	Hallucinations.
10	Circulatory collapse and heat stroke.

regular basis, as the rate of sweat loss will be affected by the ambient temperature and the nature of the session being undertaken (which should be recorded). There are various ways of tackling this but the best is to weigh on accurate scales with no or minimal clothing before the session and then after the session to remove wet clothes and dry the skin and re-weigh. Any drinks consumed during the session should also be taken into account.

Try to ensure the rower is hydrated before the session. Alcohol in small quantities is fine but avoid large amounts as this will affect hydration levels. Tea and coffee are defined as diuretics but provided they are drunk in usual quantities and not all fluid replacement is via tea and/or coffee then this is fine. There is evidence to suggest that cutting tea and coffee entirely from the diet may lead to a loss of trace elements contained in both and the anti-oxidant benefits of tea will be lost.

What to Drink and When

Water alone or low-calorie squash is good for rehydration but there will be a tendency for the kidneys to excrete the water so this is good with a salty snack or meal following the session. Drinks with 3.0–6.0g of CHO per 100ml fluid will maximize hydration, provide energy for the session and aid muscle and liver glycogen storage. This level of CHO will help to keep the immune system healthy. There are a lot of products on the market that brand themselves for different purposes; if being used during a session ensure that they contain enough CHO according to the requirements of the individual and the session. Drinks high in CHO can also be diluted as long as they are not diluted beyond the point of containing 3.0g of CHO per 100ml. Commercial drinks will also contain potassium and sodium. (As indicated previously, sodium encourages the body to continue to hydrate whereas water alone often

discourages full hydration and activates the kidneys.)

Race Days
On race days make a plan that includes when and what to eat and drink to maximize performance and, if applicable, recovery between rounds. High glycaemic index foods should be included in the morning meal and for recovery. However, if the racing is spread across the whole day try to plan times in the day when low-to-medium glycaemic foods can be part of the diet.

Hygiene

Water bottles should be washed and treated with a sterilising agent regularly or, if made from a suitable material, they can be sterilized in a microwave oven or put into the freezer. Some plastics become toxic in a microwave so ensure that the bottle is made of the right type of plastic to undertake this process. Using a dirty water bottle can lead to gastric problems and if the weather is hot and/or glucose or protein drinks are being used there is a greater risk of bacterial growth.

EXAMPLE: RECORDING AND MONITORING FLUID LOSS

Here is some typical data you might record to help you monitor hydration levels:

Type of session:	Low-intensity aerobic training.
Session duration:	90 minutes.
Temperature:	24°C.
Pre-session weight:	80kg.
Post-session weight:	79kg.
Fluid taken:	0.5kg or 0.5 litres of water.
Sweat rate:	1.5 litres per 90 minutes = 1 litre per hour.

The rower should aim to replace 80 per cent of sweat lost during the session so the rower in the example shown here should be drinking 1.2 litres of fluid in this session. During and after the session in total they should aim to drink 150 per cent of the amount of fluid lost, so ideally the rower in this example will take in 2.25 litres of fluid during and after the session. (The extra fluid is necessary because the kidneys continue to produce urine.)

RECIPE FOR A HOMEMADE SPORTS DRINK

Mix together the following:

- 50ml Ribena or 50ml High Juice*
- 450ml water
- A pinch of salt

The Ribena will deliver 6.3g CHO per 100ml and the High juice 4.3g. They will also deliver potassium and sodium and so are very suitable non-specialist substitutes to drink in training.

*Other brands with equivalent contents may be used.

Monitoring

In order to gauge if you are dehydrated you can monitor the colour of your urine. There are colour charts available to show you the colour range and the relative state of dehydration. These can be very helpful for assisting rowers to remain hydrated.

Monitoring on a daily basis to assess readiness to train is a good idea, whether for serious trainers or recreational rowers. Monitoring daily waking heart rate (beats per minute), dehydration via urine colour and using a simple scale of mood will give a good indication of a rower's readiness to train. Once the baseline in heart rate has been established then any variations by ten beats or more should give a warning flag that training may need to be curtailed or stopped. Individual variations in heart rate will occur through different training modalities and a waking heart rate may be raised by five or six beats a minute following a late-night weights session, for example. Lifestyle can also affect waking heart rate, with alcohol or high levels of caffeine all making an impact. Regular monitoring will enable the rower to know exactly the status of their body and readiness to train.

Readiness to train and mood are subjective markers which have been shown to be very accurate if used on a regular basis and recorded accurately by the rower. The question the rower should ask themselves is, 'How ready am I to try today?' The results from such monitoring can also provide a very effective record of rest and recovery cycles.

Managing Winter Illnesses

Colds and influenza are a hazard of the winter months but this can lose the rower valuable winter training time, so simple precautions can be used to try to avoid winter illnesses. Colds and 'flu are caused by viruses, and colds generally affect above the neck with a slow onset of symptoms. Influenza affects below the neck and is usually accompanied by a fever and muscle and joint pain.

Viruses are spread through contact with contaminated surfaces or people and generally enter the body through the eyes, nose, mouth or respiratory tract. Avoiding people with a cold or 'flu and careful hand washing throughout the day can help the rower to remain virus free. After exercise the body's immune system is suppressed for a time so this is a period when the rower is more susceptible to becoming ill. A healthy and balanced diet that includes all the nutrients, vitamins and minerals required can also help to reduce the possibility of virus transmission. Hydration levels also affect the body's ability to resist infections – another reason to make sure you are hydrated.

If your morning monitoring has shown that you are feeling blow par and your heart rate is elevated then you should review your training. If your heart rate is marginally raised and this is not explained by the previous day's training or lifestyle stressors then moderating the training to a less intense session may be advisable. If the heart rate is significantly raised then it is advisable to stop training.

If you do get ill with a cold or influenza, both of which are viruses, then you can relieve the symptoms but there is no choice but to let them take their course. Try to avoid contact with others as they will be susceptible to your infection. If you are likely to be entering competitions when you are ill, then you should withdraw.

Rest and Recovery

High-performing rowers sometimes refer to their rest and recovery time as a training session because they know that during this time while the body is resting and recovering it is getting 'stronger and fitter'. In the same way that nutrition will help to deliver a performance so will rest and recovery. The amount of sleep required is very individual but a rower in a heavy training period will need more sleep and recovery time than usual. If training once a day then good nutrition and a good night's sleep is sufficient but if training two or more times a day then recovery strategies such as nutrition and rest time need to be accommodated.

Try to ensure you have good habits before going to bed, such as not eating or taking in any caffeine too close to bedtime. A regular bedtime and wind-down routine will be very beneficial – so no electronic devices, which can often overstimulate the brain. If you have the time and need to recover by sleeping in the day try to limit your sleep to 30 or 90 minutes as this is linked to the body's circadian rhythms.

PART V
STRENGTH AND CONDITIONING

CHAPTER 11

BUILDING AND TRAINING THE ROBUST ROWER

All rowing, no matter the type or amount undertaken, will require an appropriate level of 'fitness'. The word fitness is often overused and ill defined but in this context it means 'fit for purpose'. If you wish to keep fit by rowing regularly for one hour at low intensity or your goal is a 1,000m race then the requirements on the body to achieve this must be reflected in the training. The demands on the body include the robustness to sit correctly in the boat and to transfer the power from the legs, trunk, shoulders and arms to the blade. Flexibility, stability and strength are the key elements required to row the boat effectively. There are different testing and training methods both on land and water that can be used to measure and then achieve these components. Chapter 9 discussed how to set goals and this chapter focuses on forming a programme capable of achieving these goals.

Posture

Good posture and the maintenance of it during the whole of the rowing stroke is really important. Efficient technique relies upon the rower being able to transfer their power to the blade and this can only be achieved with the right posture. Correct posture requires flexibility to get into the right positions and core strength to transfer power – the kinetic chain from footplate to handle.

Flexibility

In a rowing boat or on an ergometer a certain amount of flexibility is required in order to achieve effective catch, drive, finish and recovery positions. If the rower is not flexible then at best the stroke length will be short or the sequencing will be wrong. Examples of this might be using the wrong sequencing with a 'lunge' or 'rush' into frontstops or the back, for example, collapsing at the finish of the stroke. Chapter 7 outlined the correct sequencing for the whole stroke. A short stroke will make it difficult for the rower to have the correct 'feel' when rowing, particularly in the first part of the stroke. If the flexibility is not there to enable the rower to get to and 'hold' the frontstops position then the timing of the entry of the blade may be compromised, as well as length. A lunge into front stops will often encourage the rower to dip into the catch with the body and this will in turn lead to the body rather than the legs leading the drive phase. This lunge can be a false economy as a dip down with the body causes the blade to rise above the water and by the time it is buried and locked

quite a large amount of the drive has been missed.

Around the finish if the body collapses then the blade may well be pulled down very early in the stroke and come out of the water far earlier than is desirable. This will lose the connection between the foot stretcher and handle, with a reduced stroke length and consequent force production.

Many rowers have short and weak hamstrings (biceps femoris, semi-tendinosus and semi-membranosus) and strong and short hip flexors (particularly psoas major). The effect of this is to pull the back of the pelvis down and the front of the pelvis up. If this is combined with poor core strength then the rower will achieve forward reach by bending at the lumber spine. The lumber spine does enable limited flexion and extension but it is not advisable to load up the back while the lumbar spine is in a flexed or extended position. The lumbar spine is probably the most vulnerable area of the spine, both for rowers and the general population. Ideally it should be in a neutral position and in line with the sacrum and pelvis.

Flexibility around the hips and ankles is important in order to achieve the catch position. The correct sequencing during the recovery is to rock over from the hips – so the hamstrings need to be long

LEFT: The outside arm inside the knees and the knees in a strong position.

The drag factors prescribed for a group of rowers to undertake tests and training will vary by nation. Countries such as Denmark leave it to their rowers to set their own resistance. A skilful rower will be able to generate a force early in the drive on a rowing machine. Generally gym rowers are not so skilful and so rely on a large drag factor to generate the force. Use too high a drag factor, however, and the technique will break down with the sequencing and length of stoke all being compromised. Select a drag factor that enables you to maintain fluency and consistency while rowing a long stroke. It is better to row with a lower drag factor and learn how to apply your power quickly rather than use a high drag factor with slow and technically poor movements.

A training programme on the ergometer can be set in just the same way as for on-water rowing. An additional training opportunity is the use of the drag factor to change the nature of the training session. Use a light drag factor to increase the leg speed and ability to connect at the start of the stroke. Use a high drag factor for sets of strokes or very short pieces. The drag factor on an air resistance machine can be further reduced by placing a bag over the whole of the flywheel complex.

Sitting Correctly

How you sit on the seat will determine your ability to row effectively and maintain correct sequencing. Put your hands on the seat and sit on them. You should be sat on your sitting bones and not on the fleshy part of your bottom. Try alternately slumping and sitting tall and tilting the pelvis backwards and forwards. The sitting bones, also known as the rocker bones, should always be in contact with the seat. As the pelvis tilts forward and back the position on the rocker bone changes but this is the part of the body that should be in contact with the seat. This is the same sitting position that should be maintained in the boat.

Testing and Monitoring Using the Rowing Machine

As well as being used for tests such as the standard 2000m and 5000m tests the ergometer can be used for physiological testing. Tests include submaximal step tests measuring the lactate levels for each wattage output. When repeated this can show if the aerobic base is improving with training. A full VO_2 test can also be carried out using gas analysis. Finally, and probably the most useful, is regular monitoring using set distances or times.

Training zones and heart rates are explained later in this chapter. An aerobic session such as UT2 (basic oxygen utilization training, see 'Training Zones' section) can be monitored either using heart rate or, if available, lactate. The rower will find that when the training aim is to improve aerobic capacity the split will go down for the same lactate or heart rate. If the monitoring is in blocks of 5k or 6k with a one minute rest to record lactate or heart rate and have a drink this is very repeatable every one to two weeks. For a UT2 session the blocks should take 20–30 minutes and there should be a minimum of two. This can also be a set time, say 60 minutes split into two 30-minute blocks, with monitoring of the split maintained and meters covered.

Be aware that the environment, the intensity of the training period and the time of day can all have an effect on the results, so monitoring should be conducted over time and not just from one session to the next. This type of testing can also be used to see how a rower has recovered from a hard training or racing period. If they are not fully recovered this may show in the first block but more likely it is in the second where they will show a deterioration in performance.

Cross-training

If you have rowers training all year then sometimes having another mode of training can provide fun and a challenge.

Rowers with limited amounts of training time can add in additional sessions by cycling to work or running in their lunch break, for example. For young people engaged in several sports their training for their other activities must be included when calculating their rowing programme.

In the winter rivers may be running too fast to row on, or they may be covered in ice, or the weather will be foggy. It is possible to have alternative training programmes that can still achieve the desired outcomes, however. In the winter the main aim is to develop aerobic capacity and this does not need to be in a rowing boat or on an ergometer. Running, swimming, cycling and cross-country skiing can all be useful additions to the winter training programme. Increasingly, military-style outdoor training is becoming popular and this could also be used as a mode of winter training. All of these activities can help to develop general fitness but be aware of the intensity and factor this into the training appropriately.

Running

Running can be a very useful addition to rowing training. Very little kit is needed and it is usually possible to find somewhere suitable to run. Ideally a good pair of running shoes rather than general trainers should be worn. These do not need to be expensive but ensuring they fit the wearer and have the right structure is essential, especially as many rowers are tall and hence heavy.

Attention should be paid as to how to breathe when running. The runner develops a rhythm, which will be something like breathing in for two strides and out for three. In the trained runner the frequency of stride does not vary very much but the stride length increases and the time on the ground decreases as they increase their pace. When running uphill strides should be slightly smaller and strides should be lengthened for coming downhill. As running is so versatile and it requires the rower to be athletic, running training in all programmes is very effective (even if this is only as part of a warm-up).

Cycling is a good cross-training exercise.

When running the heart rate will be higher for a perceived effort than in rowing and the time will be shorter than for the equivalent rowing workout.

Swimming

In order for the rower to profit from a swimming session they need to be able to swim well enough to get their heart rate into the aerobic training zones, and they will need to have the skills to coordinate their arms and legs. For most people the actual weight of their body in the water is only a few kilograms. For those who do not float well or who have poor technique the work rate required to achieve one or two lengths of the pool may be as much as they can manage and the session then becomes a series of anaerobic intervals.

Front crawl is the most efficient stroke, with the arms producing most of the forward motion and the legs contributing little to the overall speed. In breaststroke the legs contribute significantly more of the power and overall speed. In swimming

there is an additional pressure on the thorax from the water, thus exerting a stress on the ability to expand the lungs and breathe. Breathing is in time with the stroke and so this is a good discipline for rowers as it requires breath control. Swimming uses less muscle mass than rowing.

Cycling

Cycling is five times more efficient than walking. It is a lower limb activity and depending on the terrain the intensity of the training is quite a lot lower than on an ergometer or in a rowing boat. Cyclists aim to keep the pedal cadence at between ninety and a hundred per minute, as this does not build up lactate in the muscles as much as with a lower cadence and higher force.

The skills required for cycling effectively are quite different from rowing. Handling skills on the bike, etiquette on the road, riding in a group and defensive riding are all things to be considered if planning to ride in a group or on public roads. As

cycling is primarily a lower limb activity it will need to be maintained for longer than rowing or running to get the same training benefit.

Cross-country Skiing

The large muscle mass involved in cross-country skiing can make it seem much easier than covering the same distance on foot. However, the energy expenditure required to transport the body over the same distances can be the same or higher in skiing, especially if uphill sections are involved. Consistently in physiological studies cross-country skiers are shown to have the highest oxygen uptake per kilogram per minute of any of the sports. This makes it an excellent sport for developing aerobic capacity. Athletes in many Northern European countries or those with consistent winter snowfall use this as a mode of training in the winter months. Once introduced to the sport the rower can soon get a very effective workout, but it is on snow and hence requires good coordination and balance.

CHAPTER 12

PLANNING THE TRAINING PROGRAMME

A training programme should be planned with the major goal for the year as the final event. As stated previously, any goals must be those of the rower and the group but not the coach. For many rowers the end goal will be performance in a competition, whether on the water or rowing machine, but for the touring rower or explorer this may be a key activity in which they want to participate. Most competitive rowing programmes are designed annually or for an Olympic cycle but this may not be important for a recreational rower. More experienced rowers should be involved in writing their programme with their coach.

There are many ways of drafting a plan and the different types of training that can be included. Ensure you understand the requirements of the identified event and how each aspect of this can be included into a training programme. Writing a training programme is like baking a cake – if you know what type of cake you are making then getting the mix of training right is more obvious. Training sessions should include skill and technique, physiology, psychology, flexibility, core stability, strength and tactical requirements. Mental training should be included throughout the entire process. It is advisable to start planning the programme from the end of the year and work back.

Principles of Training

For a training programme to be effective there are principles that must be observed. The training session on its own does not bring about improvements but rather the adaptation by the body to intensity and demands placed upon it. The improvement takes place during the rest and recovery, which is why this is such an important part of a training programme.

- Progressively overload for gradual improvement. In order for the body to continually adapt the programme must increase in volume or intensity.
- Be specific to the activity in regard to the muscles involved, the speed of movement and the range of motion. In the preparation period this may be more general to rowing but specific to the focus of the programme at that stage (to improve strength, for example, if that is the focus). As the year progresses towards the competition period the programme should more closely reflect the elements of a successful race.
- Training should be a continuous and regular process so that gains made are not lost. The programme will have periods of rest and recovery but regular training sessions should continue. If two weeks are taken off in the middle of the year with no suitable training then the body's adaptation will be reversed for this period. This is sometimes a problem for clubs, particularly schools and universities. Equally, training four times a week for two weeks and once a week for two weeks will not be effective in producing the necessary adaptation in the body.
- Recovery and rest should be appropriate to enable the training effects (mainly physiological) to take place. World class recovery is key to developing a rower – between sessions as well as from one day to the next. If multiple sessions are undertaken in a day it is important that sufficient rest is included in the programme. Technical and mental adaptations will also be better for reflection, rest and recovery.
- A system should be in place for monitoring and evaluating the focus of the programme. Ultimately, the success of this will be reflected in improved performance.
- Although the programme must be progressive the training should be increased in a wave cycle, having sessions grouped together with light, medium and hard on rotation. This wave pattern in the preparation phase can be a weekly wave with 'light', 'medium' and 'hard' weeks.
- Considerations for each session should include the intensity, duration, volume, number of repetitions, scheduled rest, number of sets, mode and finally the type of training (continuous or interval). Examples of this are outlined later in this chapter.

Developing Aerobic and Anaerobic Capacity

Aerobic capacity takes longer to develop than anaerobic and this should be reflected in the training programme. The balance on a yearly basis will be biased to aerobic training and the long-term programme should also reflect this. If a rower has a well-developed aerobic capacity built over a number of years they will maintain this base and can very quickly get back to a good level even if they are unable to train for a number of weeks. The new rower will regress much more quickly and even a short break, such as over the Christmas period, can mean they lose the benefits of a large part of their training and almost need to start again.

Table 14   Aerobic-anerobic Balance

	10 seconds	1 min	2 min	4 min	6 min	8 min	10 min	30 min	60 min	120 min
Anaerobic	85%	65–70%	50%	30%	25%	20%	10–15%	5%	2%	1%
Aerobic	15%	30–35%	50%	70%	75%	80%	85–90%	95%	98%	99%

Table 15   Periodization of the Training Cycles

Phase	Indicative number of weeks	Main emphasis
Preparation period 1	12–14 weeks	General fitness and strength General endurance Technical foundation Mental toughness
Preparation period 2	12–14 weeks	Muscular endurance and power Specific endurance Technical competence Maintain focus and intensity of training
Pre-competition	8–12 weeks	Specific endurance Technique at intensity Maintain efficiency at rate
Competition	10–12 weeks	Peaking for performance Build race profile Racing confidence Maintain aerobic and strength capacities
Transition	Max 4	Includes summer holidays Mental and physical relaxation Non-specific training

Table 16   Data for Each Training Zone

Training zone Code	Name	Heart rate	% Max heart rate	Blood lactate (mmol/l)	Stroke rate per min.	% Max boat speed
UT2	Basic oxygen utilization training	130–150	65–75	<2.0	17–18	70–75
UT1	Oxygen utilization training	150–160	75–85	2.0–4.0	19–23	76–81
AT	Anaerobic threshold training	160–170	80–85	~4.0	24–28	82–86
TR	Oxygen transport training	170–180	85–90	~4.0–8.0	28–36	87–95
AC	Anaerobic capacity training	180–190	90–95	~8.0+	>36	>100
AP	Anaerobic power training				>26	>95

Table14 gives a visual representation of the percentage of aerobic and anaerobic capacity required for different duration events. For a two-minute event the anaerobic and aerobic capacity required is exactly equal. A few rowing races are 500m, but most will be 800m and more, so they will be over two minutes in duration. A training programme should reflect the requirements for the main goal and event for the year.

- Provide a variety of type and intensity/duration likely to result in more adaptation
- Maintain motivation
- Be fun

Periodization

There are four phases in a yearly training cycle: preparation, pre-competition, competition and transition. Rowing is generally a year-round activity so the phases will cover the whole of the year. For seasonal sports the cycle will contain the same phases but they will be spread differently across the year. Those rowing in the southern hemisphere and racing in the northern hemisphere and vice versa often complete two whole periodized cycles a year.

The Training Zones

The first two columns in the table shown here give the names and abbreviation of the training zones, which relate to the training effect. The third column gives heart rate ranges for each type of training and the percentage of maximum heart rate is given in the fourth column. The way to calculate these ranges for an individual is given below. Lactate levels are given in the fifth column and, for those who have access to this information, heart rate zones (the heart rate range necessary to achieve a training effect in that training zone) can be calculated from this. The sixth column gives the rowing rate for work in these areas. The rate will vary depending on the boat type but for UT2 and UT1 this should be as shown. For the higher rate pieces an eight may be two pips above this and a single two below. The seventh column gives a percentage of maximum boat speed, which should be calculated on what your maximum boat speed will be for 2000m in the summer. In the winter your boat speed will be lower due to the colder water conditions and rowers being less well trained.

Even though the training sessions are divided into specific training zones a physiological adaptation is stimulated across a range of training sessions. All training types from UT2 to anaerobic capacity training will lead to an increase in capillaries around the muscle, for example. UT2 is the most effective training type to elicit this, followed closely by UT1, anaerobic threshold and oxygen transport training.

In addition to maximizing and increasing muscle capillaries UT2 and UT1 training increase blood volume, the number of mitochondria in the cells and aerobic enzyme response. Anaerobic threshold and oxygen transport training help to improve the ability of the body to use lactate as a fuel. Increased maximum cardiac output and ventilation capacity are best developed through transport training. A more rapid use of glycogen as a fuel and better muscle and blood buffering from lactic acid are developed though transport and anaerobic capacity training. Race-specific neuromuscular adaptations are best developed through anaerobic power training.

Using Heart Rate to Control Intensity

Monitoring the heart rate will help to determine if an athlete is achieving a level of intensity in their training that is within

THE STEP TEST PROTOCOL

1. About a week before the step test the rower should complete a 2,000m flat-out piece and the average split should be recorded as watts. The following week a step test can be carried out to determine heart rate zones for training.

2. The rower completes a full warm-up including 10 minutes of continuous rowing at a low rate and effort to enable the heart rate to stabilize. Depending on the starting point this should be between about 45 per cent of the maximum watts output from the 2,000m test. Record this heart rate.

3. Select a starting point for the test. It may be possible to determine the anaerobic threshold, and this is most likely to be at 50 per cent of the 2,000m watts value. For a very well-trained individual this may be 55 per cent.

4. The rower completes three steps of 8 minutes each, starting at the lowest wattage as prescribed and increasing by 5 per cent every 8 minutes.

5. The heart rate should be recorded for the last 5 minutes of the three steps. This should be for the latter 30 seconds of each minute – so record at 3:30, 4:30 and so on every minute up to 7:30. The reason for recording during the last 5 minutes is that this gives time for the heart to stabilize at each step and then be maintained or gradually climb.

6. Once the test is complete then the heart rate should be plotted on a graph against the watts output with heart rate on the Y axis and the watts output on the X.

The heart rate will rise at a steady rate against the watts output. The point where the heart rate flattens out near the end of the test is when VO2 max is reached, but the rower can continue to increase power by working anaerobically.

This test can be used to monitor the effectiveness of the training programme to develop aerobic capacity and power. Improvements in 2,000m test score through the season will result in a higher wattage starting point for the test. This will mean that for the same heart rate the aerobic capacity and anaerobic threshold should be at a higher watts output, as shown in test 1 and test 2.

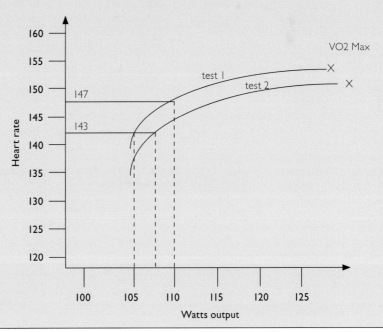

the appropriate training zone. Heart rate monitors are fairly cheap to buy and if used on a regular basis give the rower and coach a good way to monitor training loads and recovery rates. Indicative heart rates are included in the training guidelines described here (see Table 15) and for each training type. Heart rate is very individual and each rower will have different resting and maximum heart rates and a different point for the transfer between aerobic and anaerobic training.

A very crude method of working out maximum heart rate is to subtract your age from 220, so if you are 20 then your maximum heart rate would be calculated as 200. The heart rate range for UT2 would therefore be 130–150 and for the anaerobic threshold would be 170–180. For a 25-year-old this would be 125–145 and 164–174 respectively for the same training types. Owing to its inaccuracy the rower may be training in the wrong bands with the consequent lack of physiological development if this method is used, however.

Another method of determining if the rower is operating in the right training zone is to monitor their ability to speak at that level of intensity. Once UT2 training is reached they should still be able to speak whole sentences; in UTI whole sentences but with a bit more difficulty; in anaerobic threshold seven-word sentences; in threshold three to four words and once at maximal training they are unable to speak.

A slightly better method is to do a step test. This test only aims to find the maximum heart rate and from this all other phases can be calculated as a percentage. Remember that any test is only reliable if as many of the variables are controlled as possible, so for both the 2,000m test and the step test control the training and, leading into the test make the sessions lighter than normal. Environmental factors such as temperature and humidity and the time of testing are all important.

Determining Maximum Heart Rate

There is no guarantee that maximum heart rate will be reached in a 2k maximum piece so it may be necessary to use a step piece. Start at 50 per cent of the 2k watts and have four or five intervals of three to four minutes' duration with a maximum final step. Maximum heart rate should be recorded during this. As the rower becomes fitter the intensity of the work will increase for the same heart rate.

Structuring Training for Each Zone

The amount of time spent in each training zone is important and this should determine how you approach the particular training. A maximum HR of 200 is assumed for the following training zones:

1. For UT training 80 per cent of the prescribed training should be in the zone of a heart rate of 130–160. For a UT piece of work the heart rate will take a little time to get into the necessary zone but once there is likely to climb throughout the session. Try to have the heart rate near to the bottom end of the range within ten minutes of the start of the session.
2. For any anaerobic threshold training the heart rate should be in the zone of 160–170 for 70 per cent of the session. This requires a suitable warm-up, possibly with 2–4km rowing distance or UT2 paddling work as part of the warm-up.
3. For threshold training the heart rate should be in the zone of 170–180 for 50–70 per cent of the session. Again, this requires a good warm-up with a paddle as above and possibly some bursts of higher intensity.
4. For anaerobic capacity and anaerobic power training only during 5–10 per cent of the session will the heart rate be at the maximum level. Again- a good warm up is required before starting the work.

Stroke Rates and Ranges of Sessions

The rates for bigger boats such as eights may need to be higher for transport training and beyond, or on the higher side of the range given. For small boats such as singles the opposite will be true.

The reason for including a range of lengths of sessions and numbers of sets plus rating is to enable the programme to be progressed during the year. Early in the season the first UT2 session may be only 30 minutes long at rate 18 and this will be gradually extended over a number of weeks. The same principle will apply to the introduction of a new type of training or an extra session. Many sessions extend across several ranges and this helps to develop physiology while at the same time making the rower tough and able to cope with increasing workload through a piece. The perceived effort of work in a race will appear more at the same boat speed as the race progresses in line with the additional physiological requirements.

Table 17   The Number of Sessions in Each Training Zone for Each Training Phase

Training	Prep phase			Pre-competition phase			Competition phase				
	UT2	UTI	AT	UT2	UTI	TH	UT2	UTI	AT	TH	AC/P
3		2	0/I		I	2				2	I
4		3	0/I		2	2			I	2	I
5	1/2	4	0/I	I	2	2		I	I	2	I
6	I	4	I	I	2	3		I	I	2	1/2
7	2	4	I	I	3	3		I	2	2/3	1/2
8	3	4	I	2	3	3	I	1/2	2	2/3	1/2

Table 18 Sample Sessions

Training type	Session	Rate	Recovery	Boat speed (%)
UT2				
Novice or warm-up	3–6 km	17–18	None	70–75
Experienced	14–20km	17–18	None	70–75
UT1	2[3] × 20–30'	19–23	4–6'	76–81
	4–8 × 8–10'	19–23	4–6'	76–81
UT2–UT1	alternate 2–5min	18/22	None	70–81
	Total 20–48min			
	Pyramid	18/20/22/20/18	None	70–81
	8–12 × 2–4 min			
UT2–UT1–AT	2–3 × 54321'	18/20/22/24/26	3–5min	70–86
UT1–AT	2–3 × 4321'	22/24/26/28	3–5min	76–86
UT1–TR	2–3 × 4321'	26/28/30/32	10–12min	76–95
AT–AC	2–3 × 321'	28/30/34	5–7min	82–max
AT	2–4× 8–20'	24–28	3–5min	82–86
	1–2 15'–20'	24–28	3–5min	82–86
	1×30' ergo	18–20	None	82–86
TR	3–6 × 3–5'	28–36	4–6min	87–95
	2–3 (17/5 strokes × 20)	34	5–6min	87–95
	2–3 (30/10 strokes × 6)	30–34	5–6min	87–95
AC	4–8 × 250m	36	3–5min	110+
	2–4 × 500m	36	5–8min	108+
	1–2 × 1000m	36	8–10min	105+
	3 (20/10strokes × 4–6)	32–36	8–10min	105+
AP	10–20 × 10–15 power strokes 30–36 as part of a UT2 or 1 paddle			
	3–6 (6–10 × 15" on, 15" off)	32–36	5 mins	Max

The Wave Principle

Applying a wave principle to the weeks of work in the preparation period will mean there may be a 'light', a 'medium' and a 'hard' week. This variation may occur over only one or two sessions. At the beginning of the season this may be an increase in mileage or the addition of an extra session or an extra set. Remember that as the rower becomes better trained the hard week early in the programme may resemble a light week six weeks later.

A maximum effort session for any type of work should be followed by a lighter session or, for those not training every day, a day off. A maximum session is one defined as being where the load, through either quantity or quality, is at the very limits of the rower's ability. In the pre-competition period the rate and intensity of work increases. The rate should gradually come up in line with the rower's ability to adapt. While the first piece of work at a new intensity may be technically poor and inefficient initially, it should soon become competent. If it doesn't then take the rate back down and ensure technical efficiency is restored; if necessary try shorter or more intensive pieces. In the pre-competition and competition phase, spread the training so that intensive sessions are spaced across the week. For those studying or working the weekends are often key training and racing days. The main intensive sessions should be placed here to give better recovery time and most racing takes place at weekends.

Understand that when external pressures such as examinations or family issues are being dealt with the rower will find concentration and hard training a challenge. Modifying the programme may be a sensible option. Do not underestimate the effects of these external pressures.

Tapering

There are lots of ways to taper a programme. If the rowers are training every day then for one or two major competitions a year this may happen over two weeks. Tapering for two weeks before every competition will lead to a decline in training load and, ultimately, performance. These are the crews that go fast at the beginning of the season and steadily go slower from there. Even a two-week taper should not see every training session reduced. For example, in Week One maintain days 1, 2, 4, and 7 as full loads and reduce days 3, 6, 9 and 10 to quarter loads and the final two days before the event should be easy. If doing an ergo test, trails or seat racing in the club or nationally then have a mini taper with three days of tapering (so a half-load three days out and a quarter the two days before plus a recovery day after that which can be a day off or light training).

If training four days a week then ensure a similar balance is maintained so in Week One taper by tackling two or three full-load sessions and one or two at a quarter load. In Week Two then use between one and two quarter-load days and one or two easy days plus the event. This depends somewhat on where the days are in relation to the event. If too little work is done then the rower will be tapered and ready to achieve peak performance before the event arrives. Judge the mood of the rowers to see how much work needs to be maintained. Ensure that the taper includes mental preparation and racing confidence as practised in the sessions. The final two weeks should include racing pieces both to enable the crew to practise their race but also to gain confidence from the ability to execute these effectively and with speed.

Racing

There are a variety of race types. The most usual are head races and side-by-side races with anything between two and six lanes. The most efficient way to race is to keep an even speed from the start to the finish of the race. For a head race this is the way the crew should race, although sometimes if you are faster than crews around you can chase crews down or alternatively hold off. However, this should all be carried out in the context of a good start and a strong rhythm that can be maintained to the finish of the race. The shorter the distance being raced the more significant the start of the race becomes. The most difficult aspect of any race is pacing.

If racing 1,000–2,000m then divide the race into four sections. After much analysis of training strategies the fastest quarter is invariably the first, despite getting the boat going from a standing start. The fourth quarter is the second fastest and the second and third should be evenly paced. Despite this variation the trend is to more evenly pace races, with crews in some events at the World Rowing Championships evenly splitting the first and second 1000m. Find the best rate for racing by watching what happens to boat speed as the rate comes up. Early in the season the boat will be more

efficient at low rates but gradually the crew should be able to maintain this into higher-rate pieces or for a longer duration through a piece.

At some point, with the main race of the year in mind, determine the appropriate race rate by doing a series of short step pieces and seeing at what rate the boat speed stops increasing. Bear in mind that the rate may need to be two pips lower than this as you will need to maintain boat pace for much longer in the race. Use the stopwatch on a marked course to determine boat speed or the in-boat speed measure.

The training throughout the year with an increase in rating and work throughout a piece should help to develop the necessary physiology to maintain boat speed throughout the race. Make sure these pieces are completed appropriately with increased rate leading to increased boat speed. Maintain the concept of distance per stroke. Racing an even-paced race requires the crew to be confident in their plan. In most races all the crews are competitive to halfway through a race and the second half is usually where races are won or lost. This is why pacing is so important.

Strength Training

Rowing is a power endurance sport with a requirement for endurance and strength training. When these two are

developed together, both are compromised. Looking at the year the best time to develop strength is the early part of the season when the endurance sessions are shorter and less rowing-specific. Plus the winter evenings give ample opportunity to be in the gym. Underlying this training is competence in core strength, flexibility and posture. Strength can be developed by using bodyweight, so exercises such as press-ups are good for this.

Strength Exercises

- Press-ups can be progressed from having hands higher than feet to feet higher than hands, a weight or partner providing resistance, additional progressions of only one foot or one arm on the floor, and so on. The reason this is such a good exercise is the requirement of the core to hold the body in a stable position and the fact that for many people, especially women, their arms are much weaker than their legs.
- Squats are another exercise that can be used for strength training. Weight, partner resistance and variations to the exercise and the depth of the squat can all enable progressions.
- Sit-ups, curls and crunches can all be varied with weights, variable positions and partner resistance and can develop strength.

Table 19   An Example of Periodized Strength Training

Number	General	Weights	Testing and monitoring
1–4	General fitness circuit training Core strength Strength circuits	Technique only	Time the circuits ensuring exercises are completed properly.
1–6	Develop core strength	Hypertrophy/ general strength	Test at the start of the block
1–6	Develop core strength	General strength	Test at the start and end of the block
1–4	Develop core strength	Maximum strength	Test at the start of the block
1–4	Develop core strength	Maximum strength	Test at the start and end of the block
1–4	Develop core strength	Power training	Test at the start and and of the block

Table 20 Types of Training

	Hypertrophy	Strength	Maintenance strength	Power training	Muscular endurance
Load as % of 1 Rep maximum	67–85%	>80%	80%	75–85%	<67%
Number of reps	6–12	<6	4–6	3–5	>12
Number of sets	3–6	2–6	3–4	3–5	2–3
Rest between sets	0.5–1.5 min	2–5 min	3 min	2–5 min	30 sec

Periodizing Strength Training

Early in the season (for the first two or three weeks) general fitness should be the focus and circuit training can be used for this. Pick ten to twelve exercises that can be completed with thirty to forty repetitions, for example:

- three leg exercises;
- two leg and back exercises;
- two back exercises;
- two abdominal exercises;
- one arm extension; and
- one arm flexion.

This type of circuit should be continuous for 30–60 minutes and early on this may be broken up into shorter periods with a limited rest.

At the same time technical lifting can start, ready for strength development work. Early on no testing with weights should be carried out; technique is the main focus.

Key Weight Training Exercises

As with any new skill the technique must be develop first and increasing the load can follow. Pre-pubescent rowers can be taught the technique using broom sticks or very light weights. (See the explanation in Chapter 11 of peak height velocity; eighteen months after peak height velocity is when strength can best be developed.) The main lifts are the dead lift, power clean, squat, bench pull and bench press. For the more advanced, overhead

exercises such as a snatch can be added. The rower must have the core stability and general strength plus the mobility in the joints to undertake these exercises.

Monitoring and Testing

A training programme is only effective if it develops the physiological, technical, tactical, psychological and athletic abilities necessary to row. Monitoring and testing should form a key part of the training programme. Each phase should be tested to ensure the desired training effects have been delivered; if they have not then the programme can be changed. As already identified in Chapter 9 the rower should keep a training diary, and monitoring and testing should play a part in this.

Regular monitoring will ensure the desired effects of the programme have been met. In the endurance phase this will include repeat sessions, such as UT2 or UT1 as described earlier in this chapter. Regular 30 minute ergometer tests at

anaerobic threshold will show if the aerobic capacity is changing, as well as giving a good workout. If improved technique is the aim then it will be useful to use video; improvements can be monitored and when the rates increase so the technique should improve as well.

In addition to monitoring the programme regularly, testing will provide the real feedback to see if all aspects of the programme are being effective. On water tests and trails, ergometer tests and racing will all test this out. The weights periodization should include testing regimes. Monitoring and testing should lead to confirmation that the training programme is delivering what was intended. If it is not then change the programme when there are unexplained poor outcomes. Small tweaks can often deliver the desired outcome – so changing only one or two sessions a week may well be sufficient if you have followed the principles described here for writing a training programme.

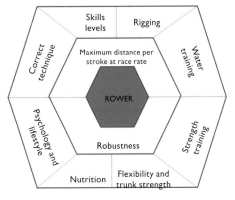

The ingredients for a successful rowing racing programme.

The starting position for the power clean and dead lifts. The hands are just outside the shoulders with an overhand grip.

The shoulders are in front of or level with the bar. The feet are beneath the bar and the shins are in contact with the bar. The weight is on the heels. Ensure there is no slack in the system by pulling on the bar slightly – checking 'the kinetic chain'.

The dead lift

Push down through the feet.

Maintain an angle between the floor and back until the bar has reached the knees.

Push the hips forward. The upper back remains straight throughout the lift.

The power clean

As for the dead lift, but continue to push the feet through the floor and be explosive in moving the bar from the knee to the hip.

Move into a jumping position while maintaining straight arms.

Perform a powerful jump while keeping the bar close to the body and shrug the shoulders to keep the bar moving upwards.

Drop under the bar once at a suitable height.

Catch the bar on the shoulders.

Swiftly rotate the elbows forward to a horizontal position.

The squat

Place the bar on squat stands and step forward into the bar.

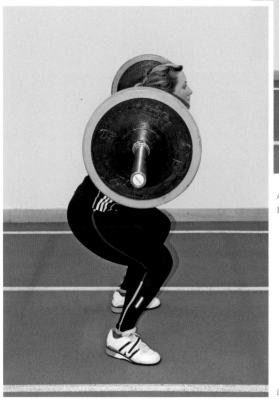

ABOVE: Keep the back flat with the feet at least shoulder width apart and the toes turned slightly out.

LEFT: Keep the back flat and heels on the floor during the descent.

A half squat is when the knees are at right angles.

ABOVE: Drive up, straightening the knees and the hips at the same time and stand up straight at the end of the lift.

LEFT: A parallel squat is when the top of the thighs are parallel with the floor (a deep squat is below this but you must keep the back flat and weight on the heels).

The bench pull

Ensure the body is lying flat on the bench and the weight is resting on the ground or a support when the arms are straight. Use an overhand grip.

Set the shoulder blades and pull on the bar, ensuring the shoulder blades move around the ribcage.

Ensure the body and head stay in alignment throughout the lift.

At the top of the lift touch the bench with the bar and ensure the elbows remain above the bar.

The bench press

Use a stand to hold the weight. Ensure the body is flat with the feet on the floor and the lumber spine in neutral. If using a heavy weight use a spotter to guide the bar on and off the stand and to help if the weight becomes too heavy.

Use an overhand grip and place the hands wider than shoulder width apart.

Control the speed of the bar down and bring the bar down to the body.

During the drive phase push up with the arms while maintaining neutral spine position and keeping the feet flat on the floor.

GLOSSARY OF ROWING TERMS

adaptive rowing   See Paralympic rowing.

back down   Term used to describe using a reverse rowing action to manoeuvre the boat backwards or for turning.

backrigger   A rigger that attaches to the boat behind the rower(s).

backstay   The back brace of a *rigger* that locks the *pin* in position to maintain *stability*.

backstops   The end of the slide nearest the *bow*. This prevents the seat from running off the *slide*. It is also used to describe the position at which the athlete sits with their legs straight and the *blade* to their chest.

beginning   The moment at which the *spoon* of the blade is immersed in the water and propulsive force applied. Immersion and force application should be indistinguishable actions. Also called the *catch*.

blade   An *oar*.

bow   The front end of the boat that travels through the water first. This can also refer to the rower who sits nearest the bow.

bow ball   A ball-shaped safety cap that sits over the bow end of the boat. Compulsory on all rowing boats for the safety of other water users.

bow side   No longer used, see *starboard*.

breakwater   The 'V'-shaped covering positioned behind the bowman that separates the canvas from the stateroom. It will stop water running along the canvas and into the boat.

bumping race   Races that generally take place on small rivers where multiple boats set off at a fixed distance apart and chase each other down. It is called bumping as you achieve a bump when you catch the crew in front.

buoyancy chambers   Sealed chambers that should enable the boat to stay afloat even when swamped with water.

burst   A small number of strokes (usually less than a minute) taken at full pressure in training.

button   The plastic circular section of the oar that is pressed against the *swivel* when rowing.

canvas   The covered section of the boat that is from the *bow and stern* to the stateroom. Often used to describe how much a race was won or lost by.

catch   See beginning.

cleaver   A type of blade that has a *spoon* in the shape of a 'meat cleaver'. Also known as a big blade or hatchet.

clinker   A method for building boats using overlapping planks of wood on the hull.

collar   Plastic sleeve fixed to the oar that the *button* circles. The button can be moved along the collar to adjust blade gearing.

'Come forward'   Verbal instruction used by the cox or athlete to bring the crew to *frontstops* position ready to row.

connection   Used to describe the link between the power of an athletes legs to the force applied to the *spoon* of the *blade*.

coxing commands   Orders issued by the cox to control the rowers in the boat.

coxless   A boat without a *cox*.

coxswain   A person who steers the boat by means of strings or wires attached to the *rudder*. They can be positioned in either the *stern* or *bow* of the boat. They are sometimes referred to as the cox.

crab   When the *oar* becomes caught in the water causing the rower to have difficulty extracting the blade. The blade may strike the rower or stop the boat.

double   A boat for two *scullers*.

'Easy oar/off'   Verbal instruction given by a cox or athlete for the crew to stop rowing.

eight   A boat for eight *sweep* rowers. This boat will always have a *cox*.

ergometer   An indoor rowing machine used for training and racing, often abbreviated to 'ergo'. Many types of machines are now available.

Explore Rowing   A programme designed to get more adults into rowing regularly.

extraction   The removal of the blade from the water by application of downward pressure to the blade handle. In sweep rowing this is done with the outside hand on the blade handle. Movement is easiest when force is applied to the spoon of the blade until the last moment.

feather   This is the position of the *blade* spoon for the recovery section of the stroke, where it is flat to the water. Athletes must be careful to fully extract the blade before feathering.

fin   A piece of metal or plastic attached to the underside of the boat towards the *stern*. Provides directional stability by preventing sideways slippage.

finish   The last part of the stroke, where the blade handle is drawn in to the body. Following this (assuming clean *extraction*)

the boat will be at its maximum speed. Force must be applied to the *spoon* right to the finish so that water does not catch up with the it.

firm   A term used to suggest that the athlete is applying full pressure to the power phase of their rowing stroke.

fixed seat   Either a description used to differentiate a boat without a sliding seat mechanism or the technique where the athlete rows using arms and/or body only (therefore not moving their seat).

footplate   The shoes attach to this and it goes onto the foot stretcher. In the coxless boat the steersman's shoe and footplate enable the rudder lines to be attached to the shoe with limited movement of the toe to starboard and port thus enabling the rudder to be moved. The footplate enables the feet to be moved higher and lower.

four   A boat for four *sweep* rowers. Can be coxed or coxless.

frontstop   The end of the slide nearest the *stern*, which prevents the seat from running off the slide. Also used to describe the position at which the athlete sits with their legs at 90 degrees and the blade *spoon* at the furthest point to the bows.

gate   The metal bar, tightened by a screw that closes over the *swivel* to secure an oar in place.

gearing   A term used to describe the ratio of *inboard* to *outboard* on the blade that determines how much power the athlete can apply through the water.

GPS   Global Positioning System – a device that enables the crew to know how far and fast they are going and for extreme challenges and touring rowing where they are.

grip   The way the hands are placed on the blade or scull handle thus providing the transfer of power from the whole body to the blade.

gunwale   The upper edge of the boat's side.

head race   A race in which crews are timed over a set distance. Usually run as a processional race rather than side by side.

heel restraints   Attached to the heels of the shoes and to the foot plate. A compulsory safety feature that helps the athlete to release their feet from the shoe in the event of a capsize.

height (of work)   A measurement of distance from the seat to the point of work at the centre of the bottom edge of the *swivel*.

'Hold it up'   Verbal instruction meaning to bring the boat to a stop quickly. Performed in an emergency stop.

inboard   The length of the blade from the end of the handle to the *button* at the point where it will sit against the *swivel*.

lateral pitch   The outward angle of inclination of the *pin* to the vertical.

length   The length of a stroke – the arc through which the blade turns when it is in the water from *catch* to *finish*.

loom   The shaft of the blade from the *spoon* to the handle.

macon   The type of blade that has the traditional long-shaped spoon.

novice   A term used to describe someone who has very little rowing experience.

oar   Lever used to propel a rowing boat, also known as a *blade*.

octuple   A boat for eight scullers, generally used by J14s and under.

outboard   The length of the blade from the tip of the *spoon* to the *button* at the point where it will sit against the *swivel*.

overlap   The amount by which the *scull* handles overlap when an athlete holds them horizontally and at right angles to the boat.

Pair   A boat for two *sweep* rowers.

Paralympic rowing   Rowing for people with disabilities. There are categories of boats for a range of disabilities.

pin   The spindle over which the *swivel* is placed and rotates around this point. Most rigging measurements are taken from here.

pitch   The angle of inclination of the *spoon* to the vertical during the propulsive phase of the stroke. This is dictated by both the *stern pitch* and the *lateral pitch*.

port   As the rower sits in the boat port is to their right. This is a nautical term which is understood by all water users. The portside blades are denoted by red tape.

posture   The position of the back and shoulder muscles during the stroke cycle.

power phase   The part of the stroke between the *beginning* and the *extraction* when the blade is in the water and propelling the boat.

pressure   The amount of effort applied by the athlete to the power phase of the stroke (usually light, ½, ¾, firm or full).

Project Oarsome   A project to get more juniors 14s and unders into rowing clubs and to link local schools with clubs.

quad   A boat for four scullers.

racing classification   See the rules for the type of racing in which you compete.

rake   The angle of the foot stretcher.

rate (or rating)   The number of strokes rowed in a minute.

ratio   The ratio of the time taken for the *power phase* to that of the *recovery* phase of the stroke. Ideally time taken for the recovery will be about three times that of

the power phase, so the ratio would be 1:3.

recovery   The part of the stroke phase between the *extraction* and the *beginning* or *catch* when the blade is out of the water.

regatta   A competition with events for different boat types and status athletes usually involving heats, semi-finals and finals for each event. Boats compete side by side from a *standing start*.

rhythm   Maintaining a steady *ratio* on the stroke cycle.

riggers   Metal or carbon outriggers attached to the outer shell of the boat next to each seat that support the *swivel* and the *pin*. There are currently several different designs of rigger from two- or three-stay metal or carbon tubing to metal or carbon wings.

rigger jigger   A small spanner used for attaching and adjusting *riggers*.

rigging   The way in which the *riggers*, *slides*, *swivel*, *pins*, *foot plate*, *oars* and *sculls* can be adjusted to optimise athlete comfort and efficiency.

rowlock   The blade sits in the rowlock, which in turn is attached to the side of the boat. This usually has a narrower opening at the top than the middle to keep the blade in place even in rough water.

rudder   The device under the boat that causes a change of direction when moved. It is linked to the cox or a crew member by wires.

running start   A racing start undertaken with the boat already moving.

saxboard   The sides of the boat above the water line made to strengthen the boat where the *riggers* attach.

scull   A smaller version of the *oar* used for *sculling*.

sculling   Rowing with two *oars*.

seat   The rower sits on a seat. In fixed seat boats this does not move. In sliding seats this moves up slides.

self bailer   A device that can be opened when the boat is moving to enable water to leave the boat (usually on coastal boats).

shell   The smooth hull of the boat, sometimes made from wood but more commonly now from a synthetic material.

shoes   Most river boats have shoes attached to the footplate.

slide   The two metal runners on which the seat travels.

span   The distance between the centres of the bow and stroke-side *swivel* on a sculling boat.

spin turn   A term used to describe turning the boat on its axis.

spoon   The end of the oar that enters the water. It is usually painted in the colours of the club represented by the athlete.

spread   The distance from the centre line of the boat to the centre of the pin in sweep rowing.

square or squaring   To turn the oar so that the *spoon* is at 90 degrees to the water. This action should be done early during the recovery to ensure good preparation for the *catch*.

staggered seating   Some categories of boat are quite short and so offset the seating to enable all the rowers to fit in the boat.

stake boat   An anchored boat or pontoon from which rowing boats are held prior to a race starting.

standing start   A racing start from a stationary position.

starboard   This refers to the left as the rower sits in the boat and is nautical terminology understood by all water users. The starboard blades are denoted by green tape.

stateroom   The area of the boat in which the rowers sit.

stern   The end of the boat that travels through the water last.

stern pitch   The sternwards angle of inclination of the *pin* to the vertical.

stretcher or stretcher bar   This is attached to the boat at the keel and gunwale to enable the rower to push off and deliver their power. This may have straps, clogs or shoes attached.

stroke   1. One cycle of the *oar*. 2. The rower who sits closest to the *stern* of the boat in front of all the others and is responsible for the *rating* and *rhythm* of the boat (other crew members can influence rating and rhythm from behind).

stroke side   See port.

sweep   Rowing with one oar on one side of the boat.

swivel   The U-shaped plastic rotating piece mounted on the *pin* in which the oar sits whilst rowing.

tap down   To the lower the hands at the end of the stroke to remove the *spoon* from the water.

tap turn   A term used to describe a method of turning the boat where each rower uses a forwards or backwards rowing action with their arms only.

thole pins   Two wooden pins attached to the side of the boat through which the blade is placed. One is generally soft wood and the other hard so the pin will be destroyed when a crab is caught rather than taking out the side of the boat.

timing   The synchronicity of the crew with each other and the boat.

trestles   Portable stands used to support a boat for *rigging*, washing, admiring, etc.

washing out   Allowing the blade to come out of the water during the final part of the drive phase.

watermanship   The knowledge of boats and local conditions together with the technical skills to propel a boat

RIGGING CHARTS

Principles for rigging	
1	Aim to enable the rower to get to a strong posiiton at the catch and finish and maintain this through the drive phase 3
2	A 55%–35% ratio of catch to finish angle will enable the rower to feel this is rowing
3	At low rates a minimum of 1:1.5 ratio of blade in the water to recovery
4	A minimum of an angle of 77 degrees for sweep and 90 for sculling
5	Only change one thing at a time so you can be objective in evaluating the effect
6	When multiple crews use the same boat, try to use different blades both overall length and spoon sizes rather than more complex rigging such as spread changes

The assumptions at the top of the tables given here are that all these factors build on each other, so for a beginner the most important thing is having sufficient angles at the catch and finish. For seventeen- to eighteen-year-old juniors and Club rowers, having a rig that enables them to maintain the right rhythm is important but this assumes that the rig also enables the rower to get the right catch and finish angles.

Rigging table for twelve- to fourteen-year-old junior rowers using Macon blades

- The most important thing for new beginners is they have sufficient catch and finish angles to get the feel of sculling or sweep.

- A small twelve-year-old will need a narrow span, so perhaps 153 with blades of 284 and inboard of 83 will give an overlap of 16cms. For a smaller person a smaller overlap will help to ensure that the angle is in the ratio of 55 per cent at the catch and 35 per cent at the finish.

boat type	span	blade type	overall length	inboard	overlap
1×	153–161	Macon	284–288	84–88.5	16–21
2×	153–161	Macon	284–288	84–88.5	16–21
4×	153–160	Macon	284–288	84–88.5	16–21
Height of feet below the seat		14–18cm smaller height for people with small feet and bigger for those with large feet			
Stretcher angle		42 degrees from the horizontal. Flatter for those with less flexible ankles and steeper for those who are very flexible and have a tendency to over compress			
Height of swivel above seat		14–17.5cm with 0.5 to 10cm starboard swivel above port			

Rigging tables for fourteen- to fifteen-year-olds using Big blades or the equivalent

- The most important thing for new beginners is they have sufficient catch and finish angles to get the feel of sculling or sweep without 'overloading' them and destroying the rhythm.

- A small fourteen-year-old will need a narrow span, less overlap and shorter blades and a taller person a bigger span and longer blades and possibly a bigger overlap.

- Ratio for catch and finish angles is roughly 60:40

Boat type	Span/Spread	Blade type	Overall length	inboard
1×	155–159	BB, Smoothie or slicks	280–284	85–87
2×	156–159	BB, Smoothie or slicks	280–284	85–87
4×	156–158	BB, Smoothie or slicks	281–285	85–86
4×+	156–159	BB, Smoothie or slicks	280–284	85–87
2–	85–86	BB, Smoothie or slicks	370–374	115
2+	86–87	BB, Smoothie or slicks	370–374	116
4–	84–85	BB, Smoothie or slicks	370–374	114
4+	85–86	BB, Smoothie or slicks	370–374	114
8+	83–84	BB, Smoothie or slicks	370–374	113

Rigging tables

A comparison of rigging for a single/pair by height.

Height in cm	Span	Spread	Sculling blade length	Sweep blade length
155–165	152–154	82–83	280–284	368–370
166–175	154–156	83–84	284–286	370–372
176–185	156–158	84–85	286–288	372–374
186–195	158–160	85–86	288–290	374–376

Blades	Fat smoothie blade 5–10cm shorter than Big blade
	Vortex edge 2cm shorter than none vortex edge

Male sixteen- to eighteen-year-old juniors and club rowers

- The most important thing for older juniors and club rowers is that, assuming the rig enables them to get in the right positions, the rig enables them to row at the right rhythm and ratio both in training and racing.

- A tall junior in excess of 2m may well require a larger span such as 160.5 with 289 blades and 89 in board.

- For a smaller person a smaller overlap will help to ensure that the angle is in the ratio of 60 per cent at the catch and 40% at the finish.

Boat type	Span/Spread	Blade type	Overall length	inboard
1×	158–160	BB, Smoothie or slicks	288–290	88–90
2×	158–160	BB, Smoothie or slicks	288–290	88–90
4×	156–158	BB, Smoothie or slicks	290	87–89
4×+	158–160	BB, Smoothie or slicks	376	88–90
2–	86	BB, Smoothie or slicks	376	116
2+	87	BB, Smoothie or slicks	376	117
4–	85	BB, Smoothie or slicks	376	115
4+	85.5	BB, Smoothie or slicks	376	115
8+	84	BB, Smoothie or slicks	377	114

Female sixteen- to eighteen-year-old juniors and club rowers

Boat type	Span/Spread	Blade type	Overall length	inboard
1×	158–160	BB, Smoothie or slicks	288	88–90
2×	158–160	BB, Smoothie or slicks	288	87–89
4×	156–158	BB, Smoothie or slicks	288–290	87–89
4×+	158–160	BB, Smoothie or slicks	288	88–90
2–	86	BB, Smoothie or slicks	372	116
2+	87	BB, Smoothie or slicks	372	117
4–	85	BB, Smoothie or slicks	372	115
4+	85.5	BB, Smoothie or slicks	372	115
8+	84	BB, Smoothie or slicks	372	114

Lightweight males

Boat type	Span/Spread	Blade type	Overall length	inboard
1×	159–162	BB, Smoothie or slicks	288–290	88–90
2×	158–162	BB, Smoothie or slicks	288–290	87–89
4×	156–158	BB, Smoothie or slicks	288–290	87–89
4×+	158–162	BB, Smoothie or slicks	288–290	88–90
2–	86	BB, Smoothie or slicks	372–376	116
2+	87	BB, Smoothie or slicks	372–376	117
4–	85	BB, Smoothie or slicks	372–376	115
4+	85.5	BB, Smoothie or slicks	372–376	115
8+	84	BB, Smoothie or slicks	372–376	114

Lightweight females

Boat type	Span/Spread	Blade type	Overall length	inboard
1×	159–163	BB, Smoothie or slicks	284–286	86–90
2×	158–160	BB, Smoothie or slicks	286–288	87–89
4×	157–159	BB, Smoothie or slicks	286–289	87–89
4×+	158–160	BB, Smoothie or slicks	288–290	87–89
2–	86	BB, Smoothie or slicks	372	116
2+	87	BB, Smoothie or slicks	372	117
4–	85	BB, Smoothie or slicks	370–372	115
4+	85.5	BB, Smoothie or slicks	372	115
8+	84	BB, Smoothie or slicks	372	114

Tables showing where straws need to be placed on the boat to reach a catch and finish angle

Using the tables below it is possible to set straws on the side of the boat to get to the desired catch and finish angles.

- The measurements given in the tables refer to the distance from the pin to where the tape measure intersects the centre line of the boat.
- Place the straw on the saxboard where the tape measure crosses on the way to the centre line of the boat.

Sweep spread	78	78.5	79	79.5	80	80.5	81	81.5	82	82.5	83	83.5	84	84.5	85	85.5	86
Sculling span	156	157	158	159	160	161	162										
Desired Catch Angle																	
50	121.3	122.1	122.9	123.7	124.5	125.2	126.0	126.8	127.6	128.3	129.1	129.9	130.7	131.5	132.2	133.0	133.8
51	123.9	124.7	125.5	126.3	127.1	127.9	128.7	129.5	120.3	131.1	131.9	132.7	133.5	134.3	135.1	135.9	136.7
52	126.7	127.5	128.3	129.1	129.9	130.8	131.6	132.4	133.2	134.0	134.8	135.6	136.4	137.3	138.1	138.9	139.7
53	129.6	130.4	131.3	132.1	132.9	133.8	134.6	135.4	136.3	137.1	137.9	138.7	139.6	140.4	141.2	142.1	142.9
54	132.7	133.6	134.4	135.3	136.1	137.0	137.8	138.7	139.5	140.4	141.2	142.1	142.9	143.8	144.6	145.5	146.3
55	136.0	136.9	137.7	138.6	139.5	140.3	141.2	142.1	143.0	143.8	144.7	145.6	146.4	147.3	148.2	149.1	149.9
56	139.5	140.4	141.3	142.2	143.1	144.0	144.9	145.7	146.6	147.5	148.4	149.3	150.2	151.1	152.0	152.9	153.8
57	143.2	144.1	145.1	146.0	146.9	147.8	148.4	149.6	150.6	151.7	152.4	153.3	154.2	155.5	156.1	157.0	157.9
58	147.2	148.1	149.1	150.0	151.0	151.9	152.9	153.8	154.7	155.7	156.6	157.6	158.5	159.5	160.4	161.3	162.3
59	151.4	152.4	153.4	154.4	155.3	156.3	157.3	158.2	159.2	160.2	161.2	162.1	163.1	164.1	165.0	166.0	167.0
60	156.0	157.0	158.0	159.0	160.0	161.0	162.0	163.0	164.4	165.0	166.0	167.0	168.0	169.0	170.0	171.0	172.0

Sweep spread	78	78.5	79	79.5	80	80.5	81	81.5	82	82.5	83	83.5	84	84.5	85	85.5	86
Sculling span	156	157	158	159	160	161	162										
Desired Finish Angle																	
30	90.1	90.6	91.2	91.8	92.4	93.0	93.5	94.1	94.7	95.3	95.8	96.4	97.0	97.6	98.1	98.7	99.3
31	91.0	91.6	92.2	92.7	93.3	93.9	94.5	95.1	95.7	96.2	96.8	97.4	98.0	98.6	99.2	99.7	100.3
32	92.0	92.6	93.2	93.7	94.3	94.9	95.6	96.1	96.7	97.3	97.9	98.5	99.1	99.6	100.2	101.8	102.4
33	93.0	93.6	94.2	94.8	95.4	96.0	96.0	97.2	97.8	98.4	99.0	99.6	100.2	100.8	101.4	101.9	102.5
34	94.1	94.7	95.3	95.9	96.5	97.1	97.7	98.3	98.9	99.5	100.1	100.7	101.3	101.9	102.5	103.1	103.7
35	95.2	95.8	96.4	97.1	97.7	98.3	98.9	99.5	101.1	100.7	101.3	101.9	102.5	103.2	103.8	104.4	105.0
36	96.4	97.0	97.6	98.3	98.9	99.5	100.1	100.7	101.4	102.0	102.6	103.2	103.8	104.4	105.1	105.7	106.3
37	97.7	98.3	98.9	99.5	100.2	100.8	101.4	102.0	102.7	103.3	103.9	104.6	105.2	105.8	106.4	107.1	107.7
38	99.0	99.6	100.3	100.9	101.5	102.2	102.8	103.4	104.1	104.7	105.3	106.0	106.6	107.2	107.9	108.5	109.1
39	100.4	101.0	101.7	102.3	102.9	103.6	104.2	104.9	105.5	106.2	106.8	107.4	108.1	108.7	109.4	110.0	110.7

USEFUL ORGANIZATIONS

British Rowing   This is the governing body for the sport of rowing (both indoor and rowing on water) for Great Britain. It is responsible for the training and selection of individual rowers and crews representing GB and for participation in and development of rowing and indoor rowing in England. The organization is committed to ensuring that the sport continues to thrive from the grass roots level right up to winning medals at the Olympic Games. Note that rowing in Scotland and Wales is governed and organized nationally (see **Scottish Rowing** and **Welsh Rowing**) but when it comes to representing Great Britain's interests to the international rowing federation, FISA, this comes under the umbrella of British Rowing.

FISA   The Federation Internationale des Societes d'Aviron is the international rowing federation. The federation is responsible for developing rowing (both indoor and rowing on water) internationally, and assists national organisations to develop their rowing. They organize a series of world championships and world rowing events each year and organizes the Olympic Rowing Regatta every four years in cooperation with the local Olympic committee.

Scottish Rowing is the governing body for the sport of rowing (both indoor rowing and rowing on water) in Scotland. It is responsible for selection of individuals for the Home Countries event and Commonwealth Regatta.

Welsh Rowing is the governing body for the sport of rowing (both indoor rowing and rowing on water) in Wales. It is responsible for selection of individuals for the Home Countries event and Commonwealth Regatta.

USEFUL WEBSITES

Association for Physical Education www.afpe.org.uk
British Olympic Association www.teamgb.com
British Rowing www.british.rowing.org.uk
British Universities and Colleges Sport www.bucs.org.uk
Canal and River Trust www.canalrivertrust.org.uk
Coastal Hants and Dorset www.coastalrowing.org
Commonwealth Games England www.weareengland.org
Cornish Pilot Gigs www.cpga.co.uk
Cornwall Rowing Association www.cornwallrowing.org
English Federation of Disability Sport www.efds.co.uk
English Institute of Sport www.eis2win.co.uk
Environment Agency www.gov.uk/government/organisations/
    environment-agency
London Youth Rowing www.londonyouthrowing.com
National Water Safety Forum www.nationalwatersafety.org.uk
Ocean Rowers Association www.oceanrowers.com
Scottish Rowing www.scottish-rowing.org.uk
Sea Cadets www.sea-cadets.org

Sea Scouts www.members.scouts.org.uk
Skiff Racing www.skiffing.org.uk
Skills Active www.skillsactive.com
Sport England www.sportengland.org
Sport Scotland www.sportscotland.org.uk
Sport Wales www.sportwales.org.uk
Sports Coach UK www.sportscoachuk.org
Sports Recreation Alliance www.sportandrecreation.org.uk
Surf Rowing League www.uksrl.co.uk
Talisker Whiskey Atlantic Challenge
    www.taliskerwhiskyatlanticchallenge.com
The Rowing Foundation www.therowingfoundation.org.uk
UK Sport www.uksport.gov.uk
Welsh Rowing www.welshrowing.com
Welsh Sea Rowing www.welshsearowing.org.uk
West of England Amateur Rowing Association www.weara.co.uk
World Rowing www.worldrowing.com
Youth Sport Trust www.youthsporttrust.org

TABLE OF VITAMINS AND MINERALS

Nutrient	Function	Sources
Water-soluble Vitamins cannot be stored in our bodies and are readily excreted		
Vitamin B1 (Thiamin)	Help to release energy from CHO. Nervous system and heart	Whole grains, nuts, meat, fruit and vegetables and fortified breakfast cereal
Vitamin B2 (Riboflavin)	Helps release energy from food. Needed for the struture and function of skin and body linings	Milk and milk products, eggs, rice, fortified breakfast cereals, liver, pulses mushrooms and green vegetables
Vitamin B3 (Niacin)	Helps release energy from food and is important for the normal structure of the skin and body linings. It also keeps the digestive and nervous systems healthy	Meat, wheat and maize flour, eggs, milk and milk products and yeast
Vitamin B6	Helps to release energy from protein and helps to form haemoglobin in blood. (Haemoglobin carries oxygen around the body)	Poultry, white fish, milk and milk products, eggs, whole grains, soya beans, peanuts and some vegetables
Vitamin B12	Important for making red blood cells and to keep the nervous system healthy. Also helps to release energy from food	Meat, fish, milk and milk products, cheese, eggs yeast extract and fortified breakfast cereals
Folate/folic acid	Needed for formation of healthy red blood cells. It is also needed for the nervous system and spedifically for the development of the nervous system in unborn babies	Green leafy vegetables, wholegrain products, liver, nuts, peats, oranges, bananas and fortified breakfast cereals
Vitamin C	Acts as an antioxidant and is important in the normal structure and functioning of body tissues. It also helps the body absorb iron from non-meat sources such as vegetables, as well as assisting in the healing process	Fruit especially citrus fruits and berries: green vegetables, peppers and tomatoes, also found in potatoes (especially new potatoes)
Fat-soluble Vitamins are absorbed through the gut with the help of fat		
Vitamin A	Important for the normal structure and functioning of the skin and body linings e.g. the lungs. It also helps with vision in dim light as well as keeping the immune system healthy	Liver, whole milk, cheese, butter, spreads, carrots, dark green leafy vegetables and orange coloured fruit, e.g. mangoes and apricots
Vitamin D	Needed for absorption of calcium and phosphorous from foods to keep bones healthy. Recent research suggests that Vitamin D enhanced immune function and improves muscle strength	Oily fish, eggs, meat, fortified cereals and spreads. Most is obtained through the action of sunlight on our skin during summer months
Vitamin E	Acts as an antioxidant and protects the cells in our bodies against damage	Vegetables and seed oils and spreads, nuts and seeds
Vitamin K	Needed for the normal clotting of blood and is required for normal bone structure	Green leavy vegetables and meat and dairy products

Minerals – There are certain minerals we need to keep our bodies healthy

Calcium	Important for the formalization and maintenance of strong bones and teeth, as well as the functioning of nerves and muscles. It also involved in blood clotting	Milk and milk products, cheese and other dairy products, some green leafy vegetables such as broccoli, fortified soya bean products, canned fish (if containing bones that are soft and can be consumed) and bread
Fluoride	Helps with the formation of strong teeth and protects against dental decay	Fluoridated water, tea, fish and toothpaste
Iodine	Need to make thyroid hormones which control metabolic processes and keep our bodies healthy	Milk and milk products, sea fish, shellfish, seaweed and iodine fortified foods such as some salt
Iron	Required for making red blood cells, which transport Oxygen around the body. Also needed for normal metabolism and the functioning of enzymes that remove unwanted products from the body	Liver, red meat, pulses, nuts, eggs, dried fruits, poultry, fish, whole grains and dark leafy green vegetables
Magnesium	Helps to release energy from food and to maintain water balance. It ia also important for the formation of strong muscles, bones and teeth	Found widely in foods, particularly green leafy vegetables, nuts, bread, fish, milk and milk products
Phosphorous	Needed for the formation of healthy boens and teeth, and for the release of energy from food	Red meat, milk and milk products, fish poultry, bread, rice and oats
Potassium	Controls water balance in our bodies and helps to maintain a healthy blood pressure. It is also involved in the normal functioning of nerves	Fruit especially bananas, vegetables, meat, fish, poultry, bread, rice and oats
Sodium	Helps regulate the water content in the body and the balance of electrolytes. Also involved in the use of energy, as well as functioning of the central nervous system	Very small amounts in raw foods. Often added during prodcessing, preparation, preservation and serving. Currently intakes of sodium are too high and so although some sodium is essential, most people need to reduce their intake substantially
Selenium	An important component of the body's defence system that protects our bodies against damage. It is also necessary for the use of iodine in thyroid hormones production, as well as the normal functioning of the reproductive system	Brazil nuts, bread, fish, meat and eggs
Zinc	Helps to release energy from food. Needed for cell division, growth and tissue repair. Also necessary for the normal reproductive development, the immune system and healing of wounds	Meat, milk and milk products, cheese, eggs, shellfish, whole grain cereals, nuts and pulses

INDEX